Welcome

To an inspirational coloring book for everyone

By Nataly Star

RECOMENDATIONS

- Begin coloring from the center outward or in any pattern that feels right to you.
- As you apply each stroke, focus your attention on the movement of your hand and the texture of the paper.
- Notice the sensation of the coloring tool on the paper, the colors blending or contrasting, and the coloring coming to life.
- Breathe slowly and rhythmically as you color, matching your breath to your strokes. Inhale as you move your coloring tool in one direction and exhale as you move it in another.
- If your mind starts to wander or you become distracted, gently bring your focus back to the coloring process.

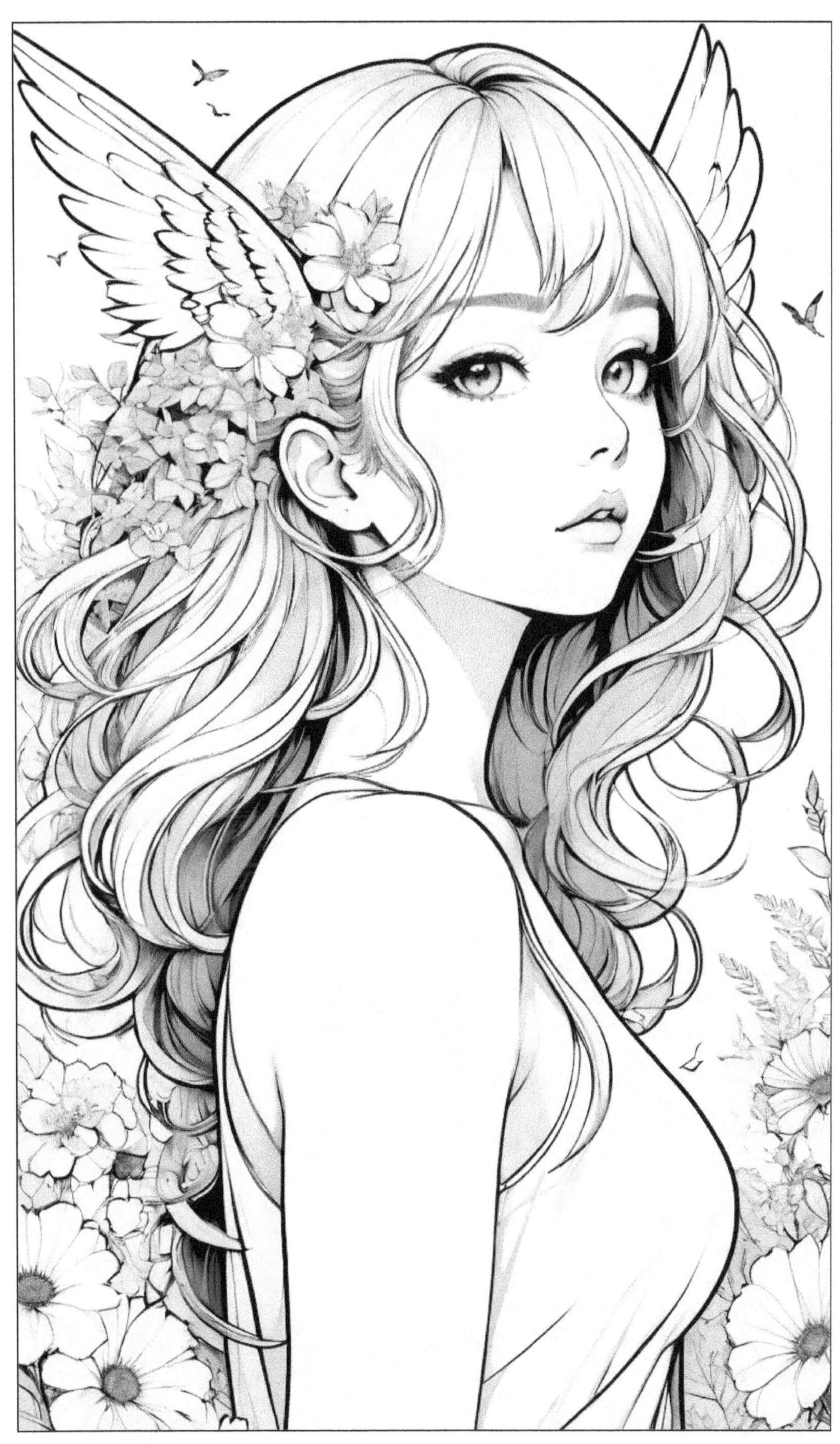

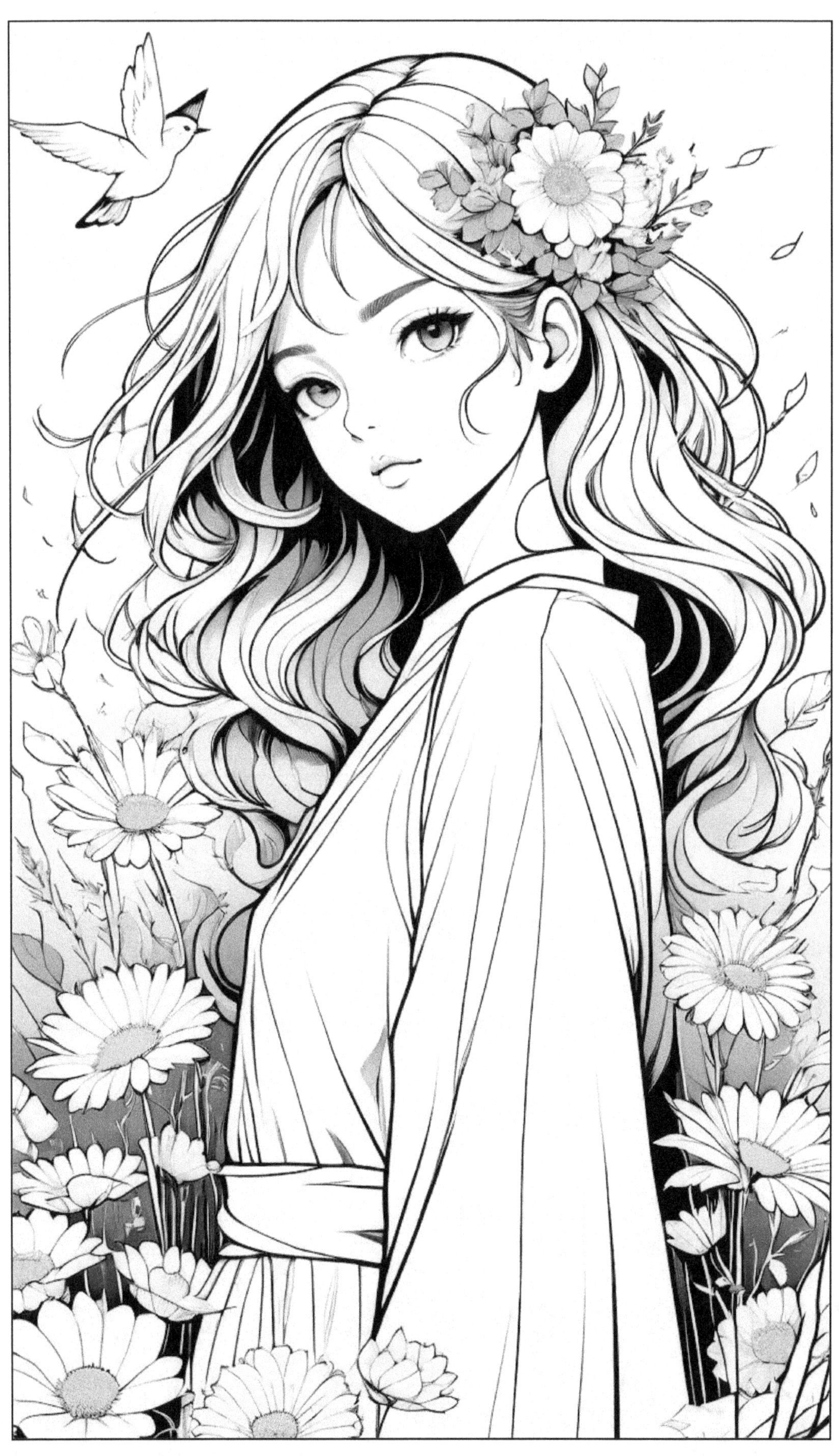

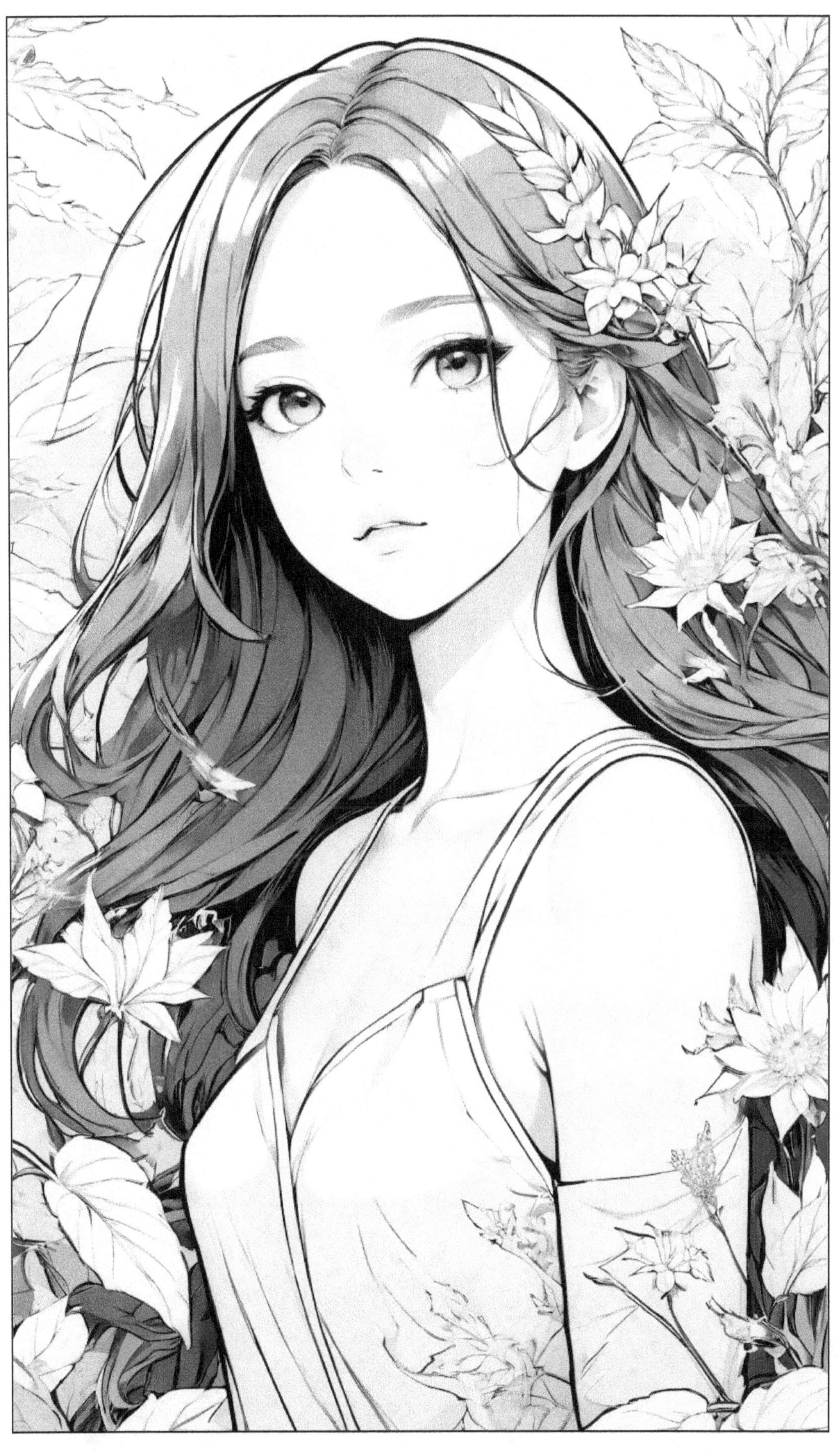

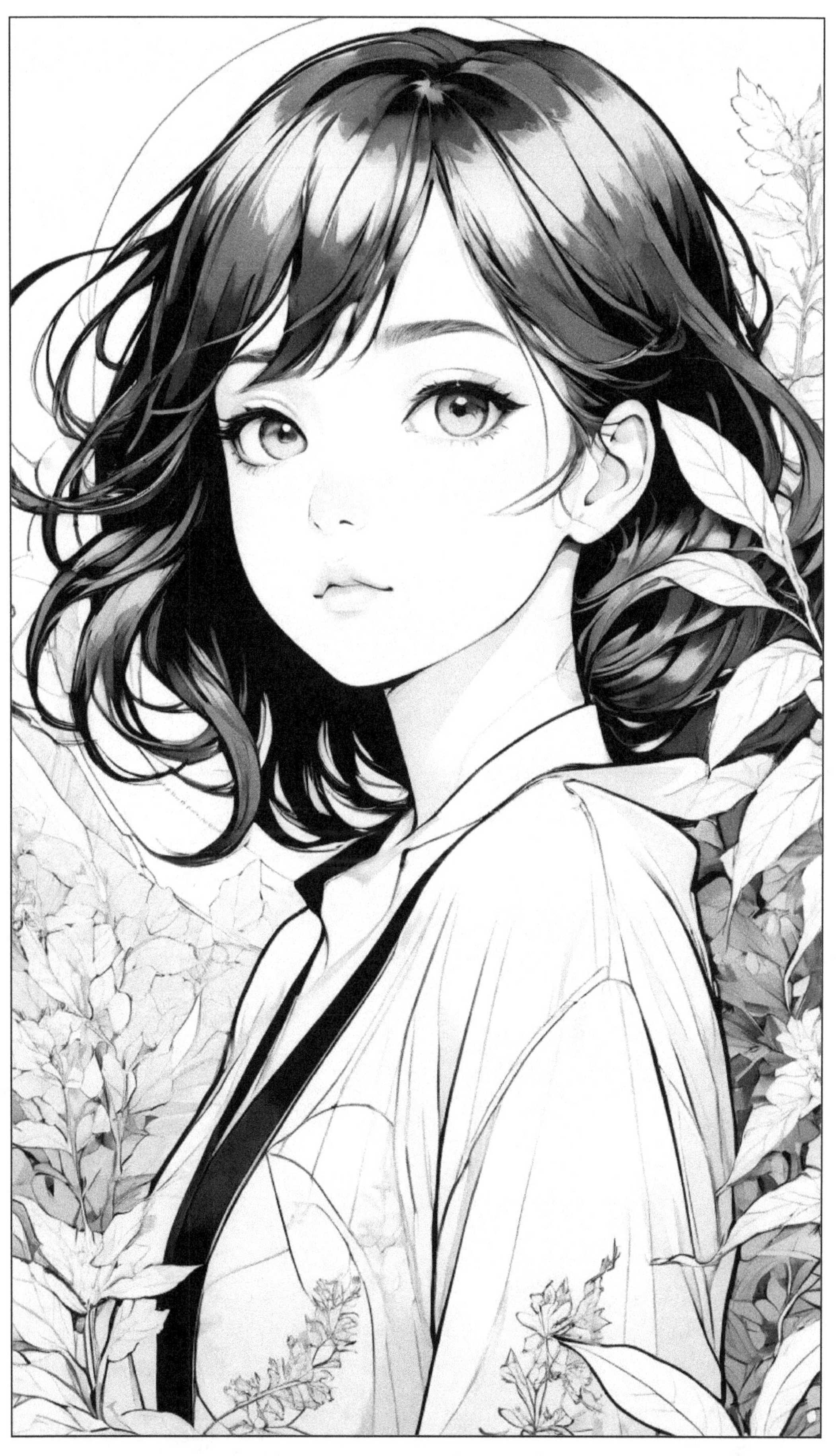

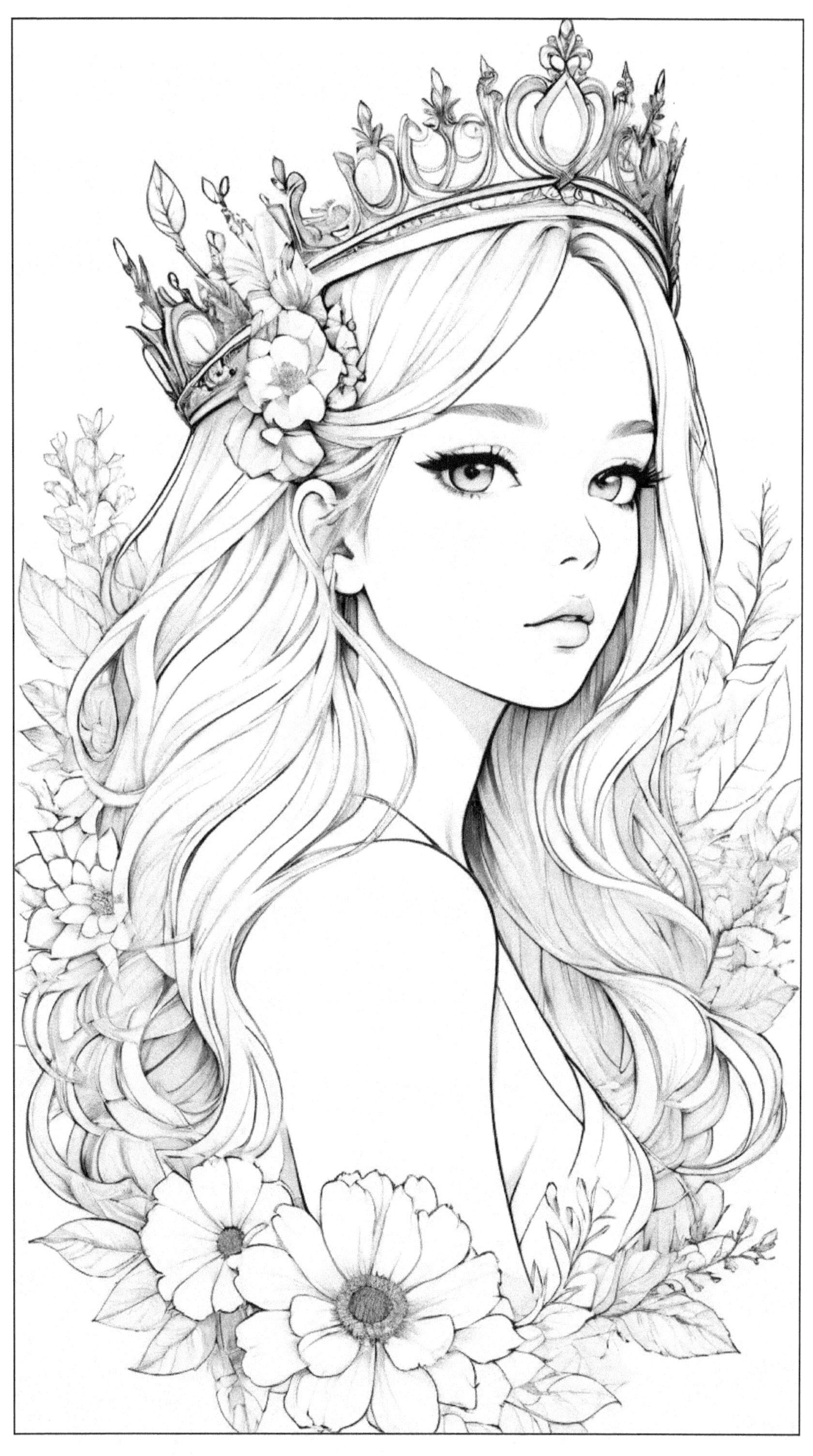

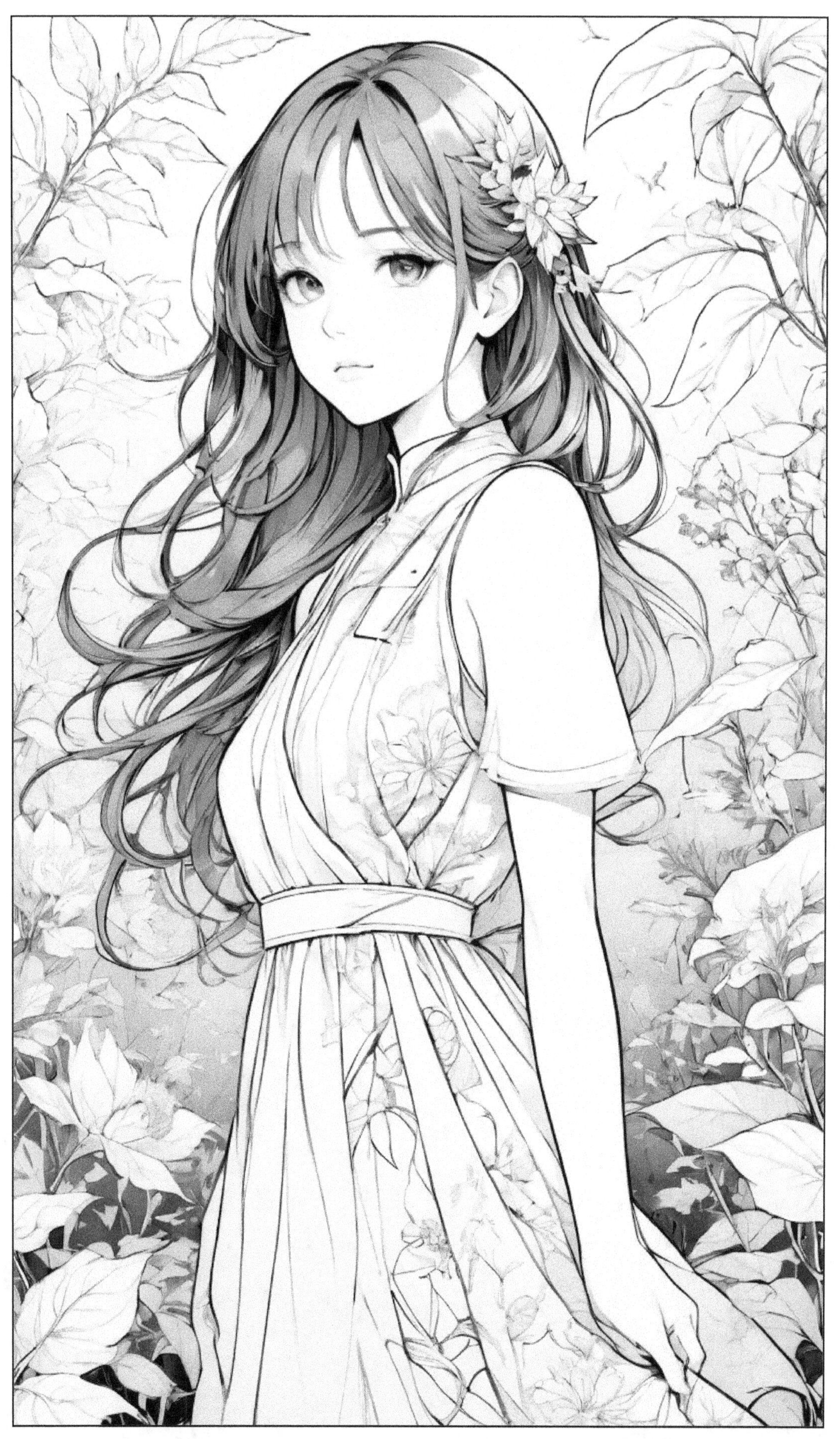

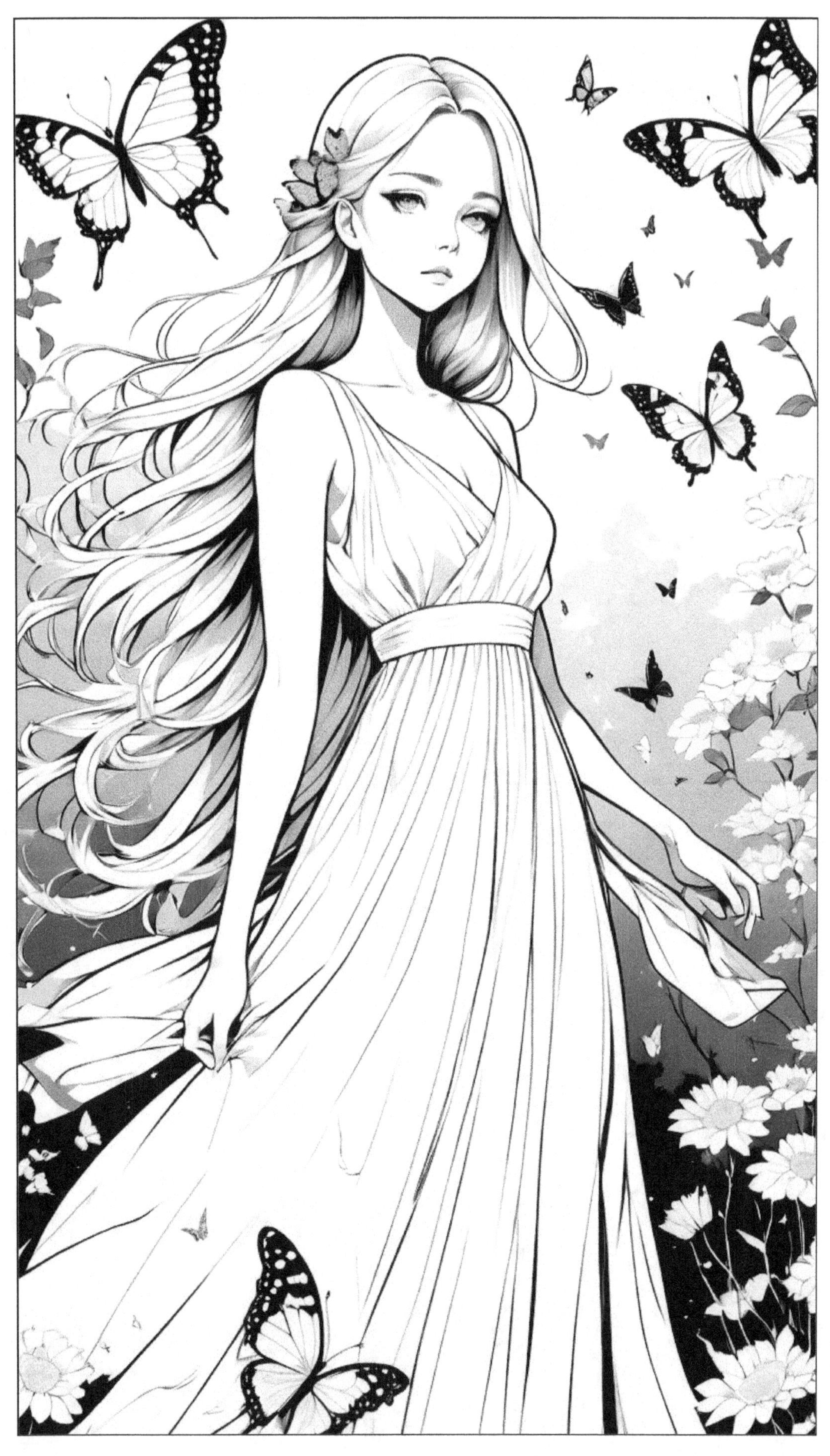

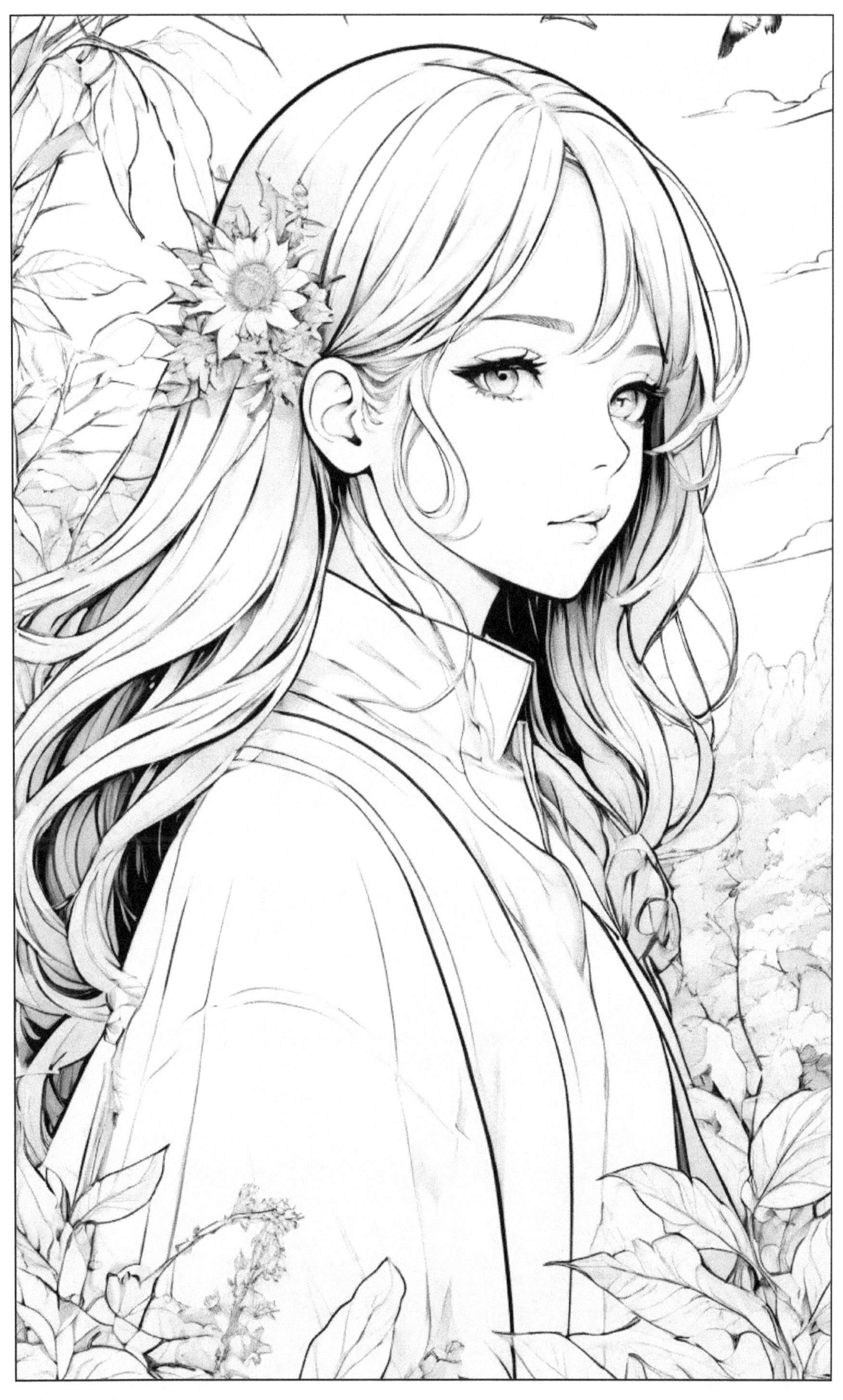

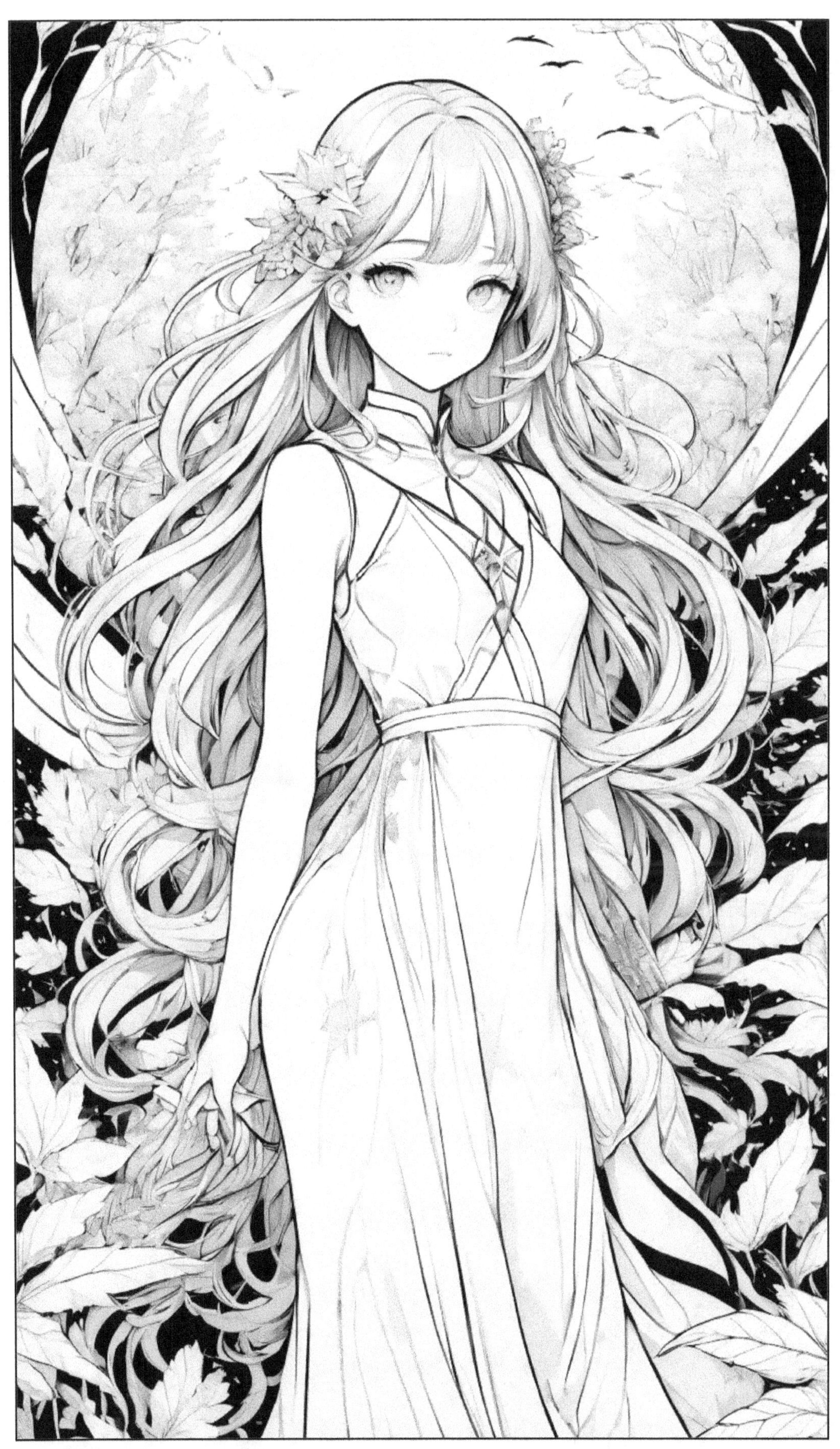

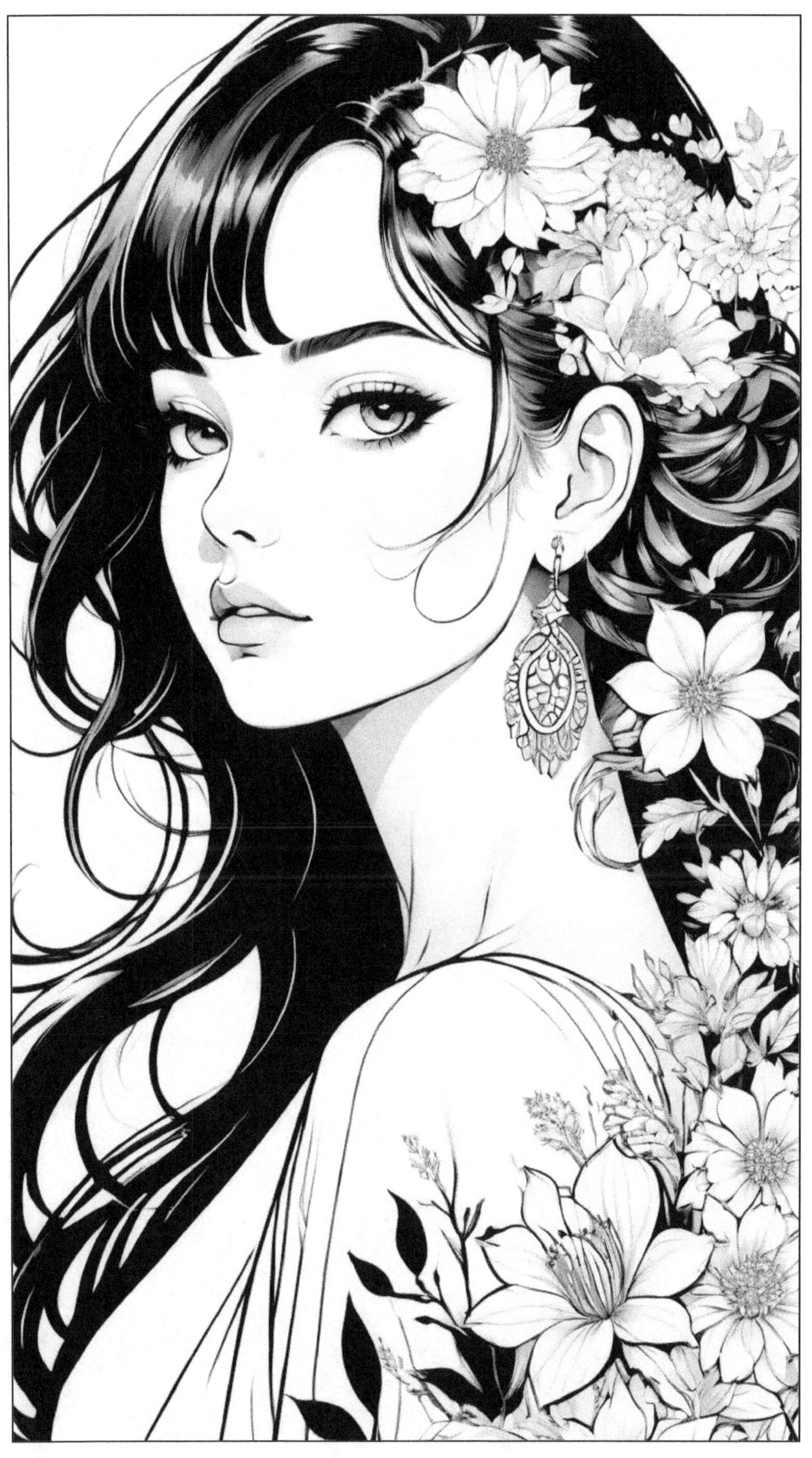

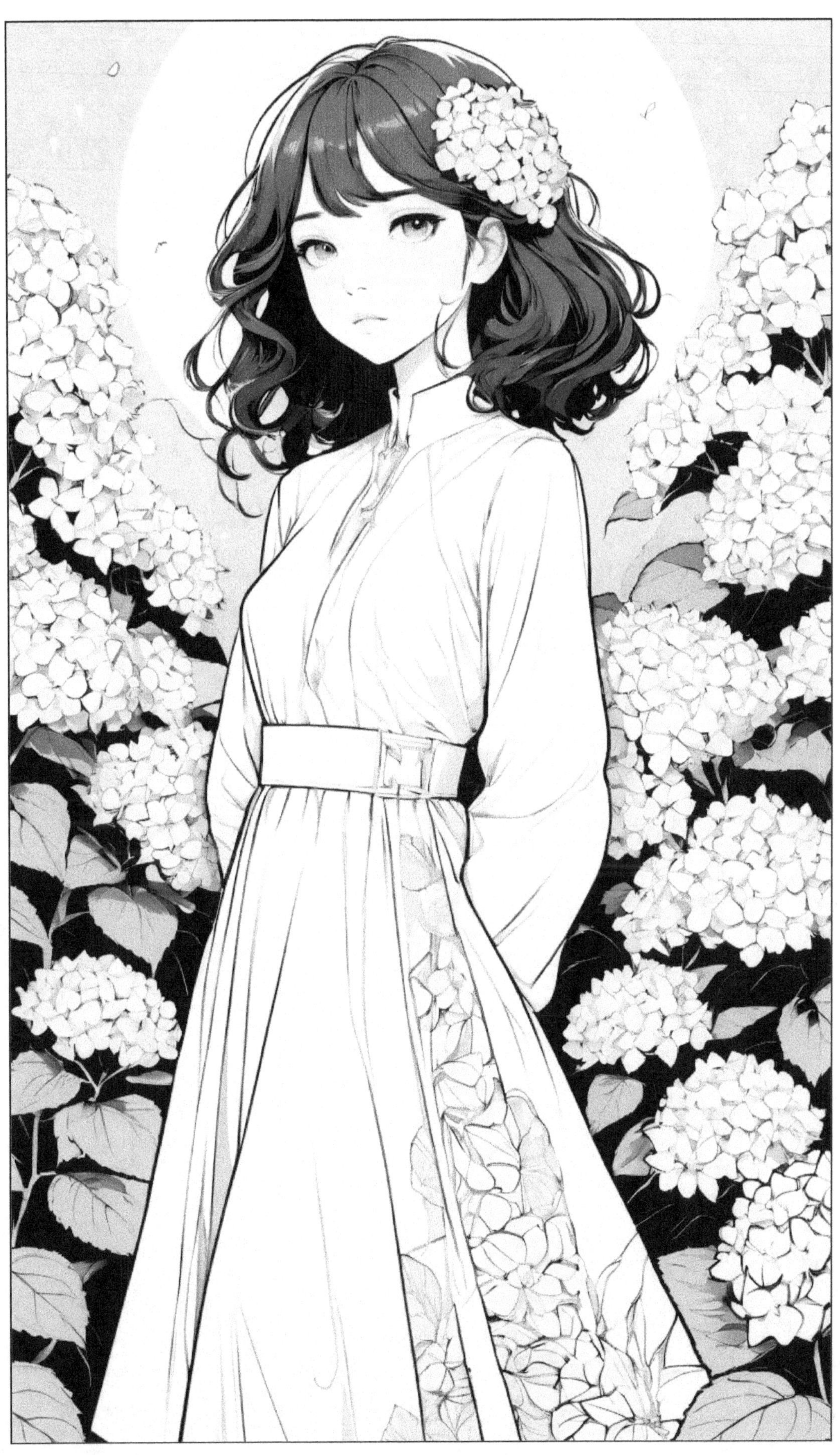

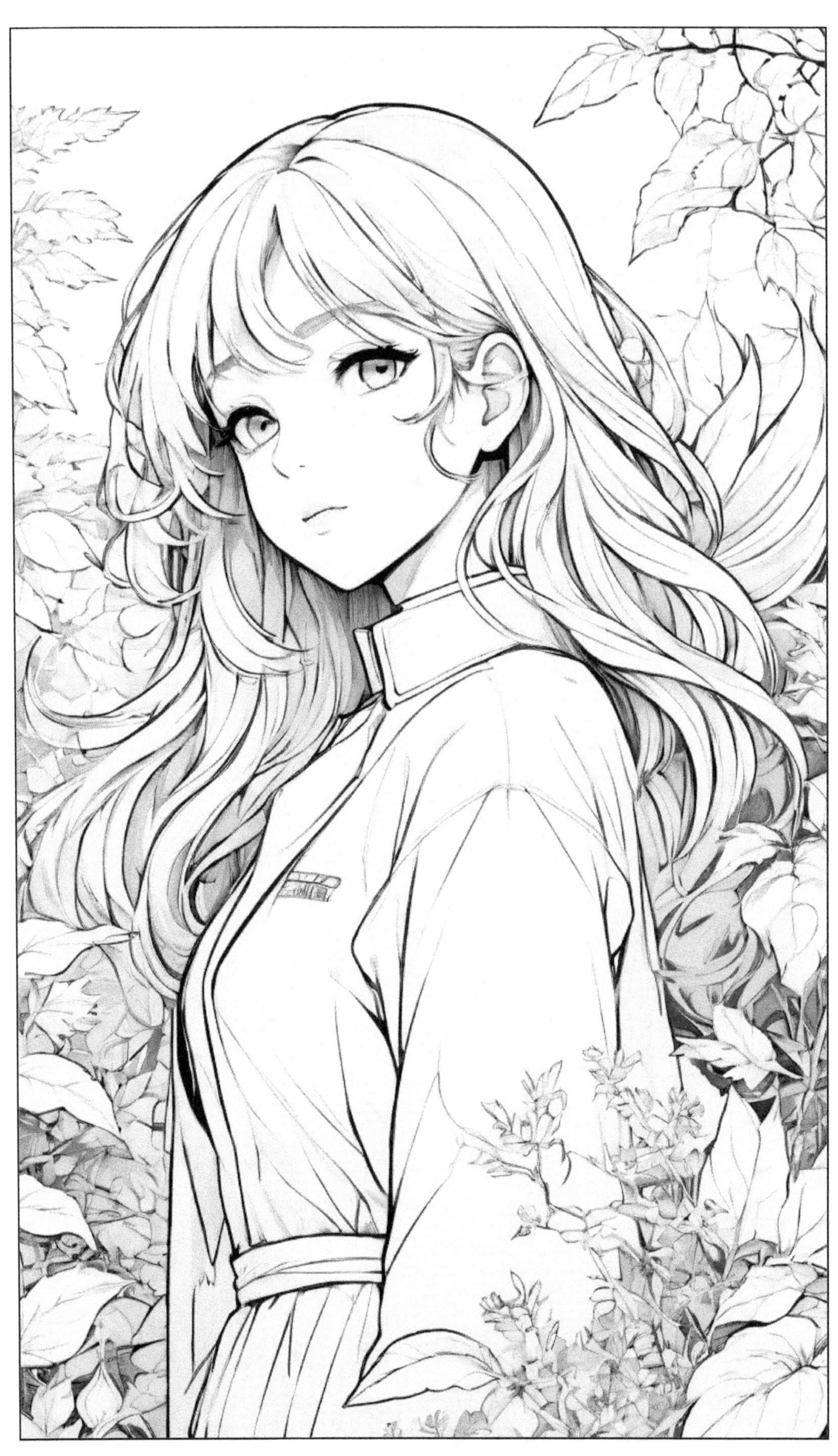

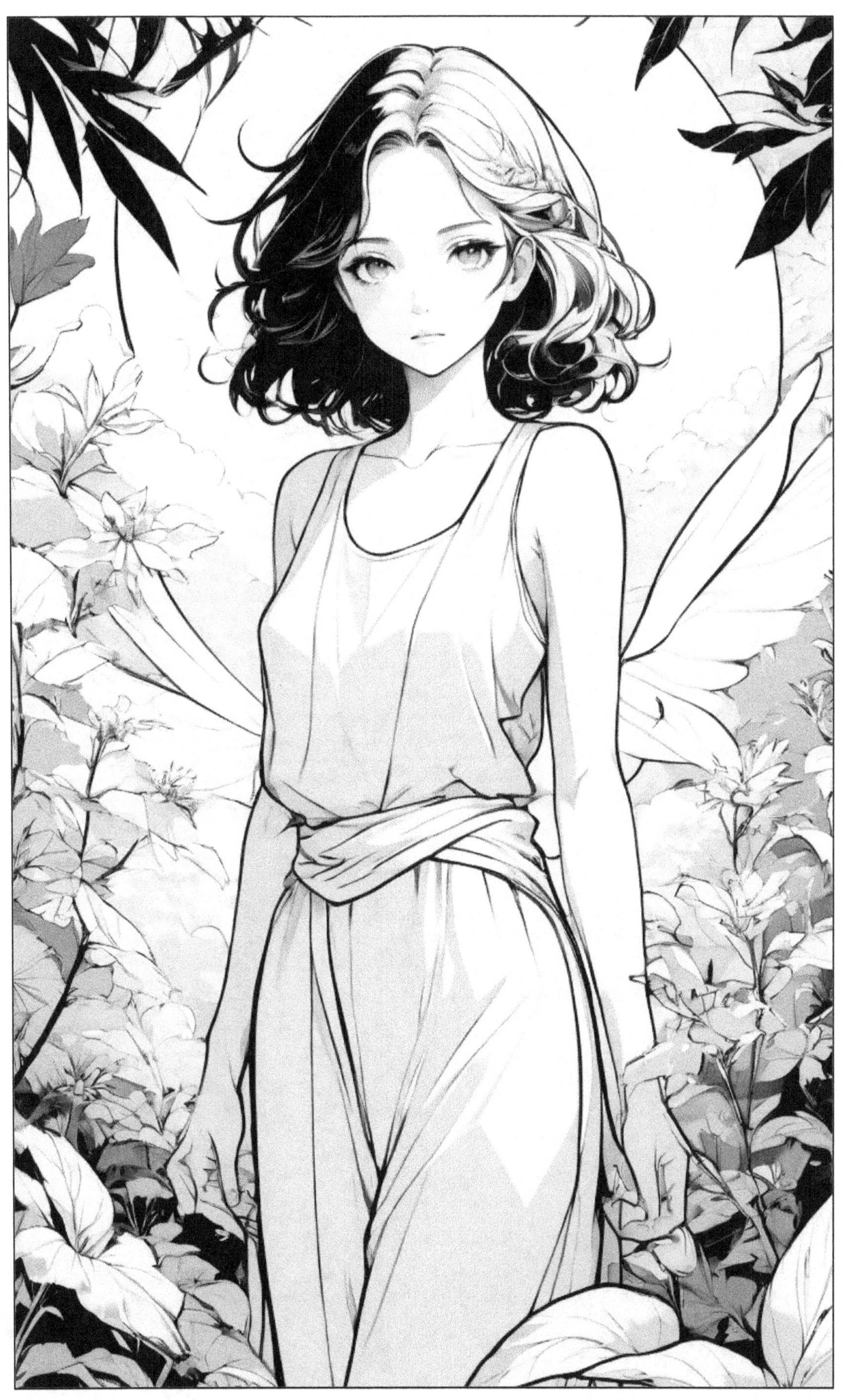

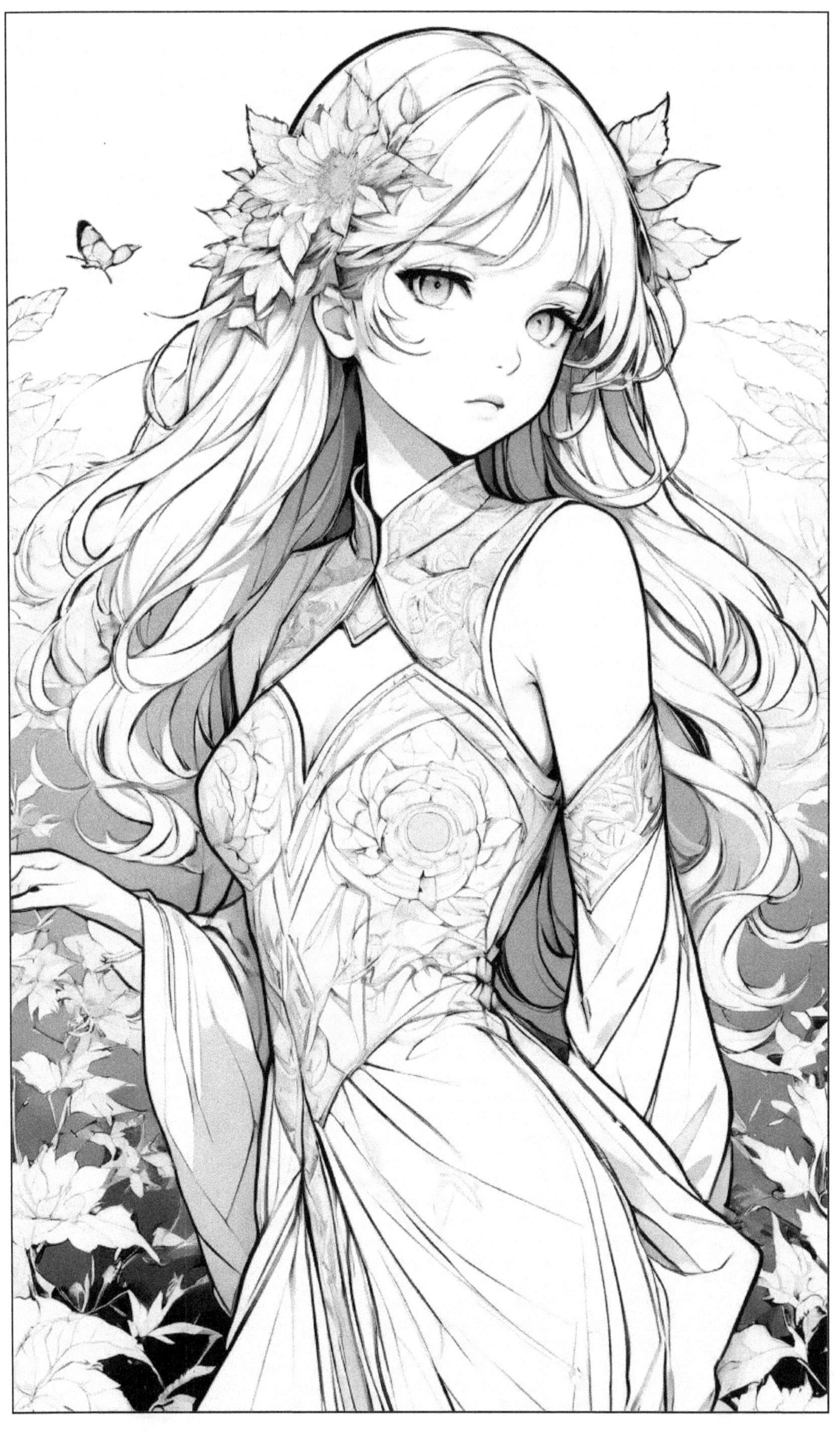

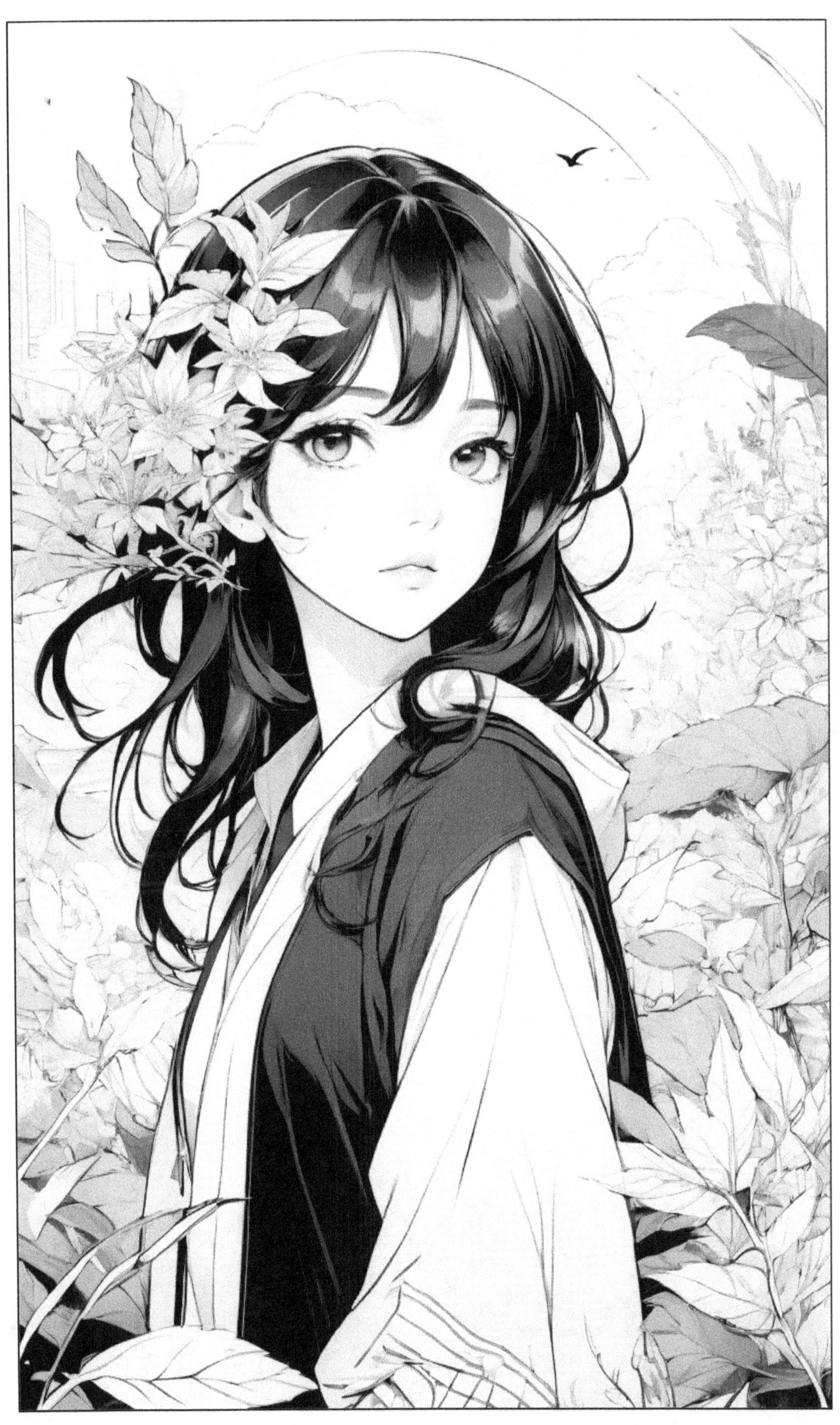

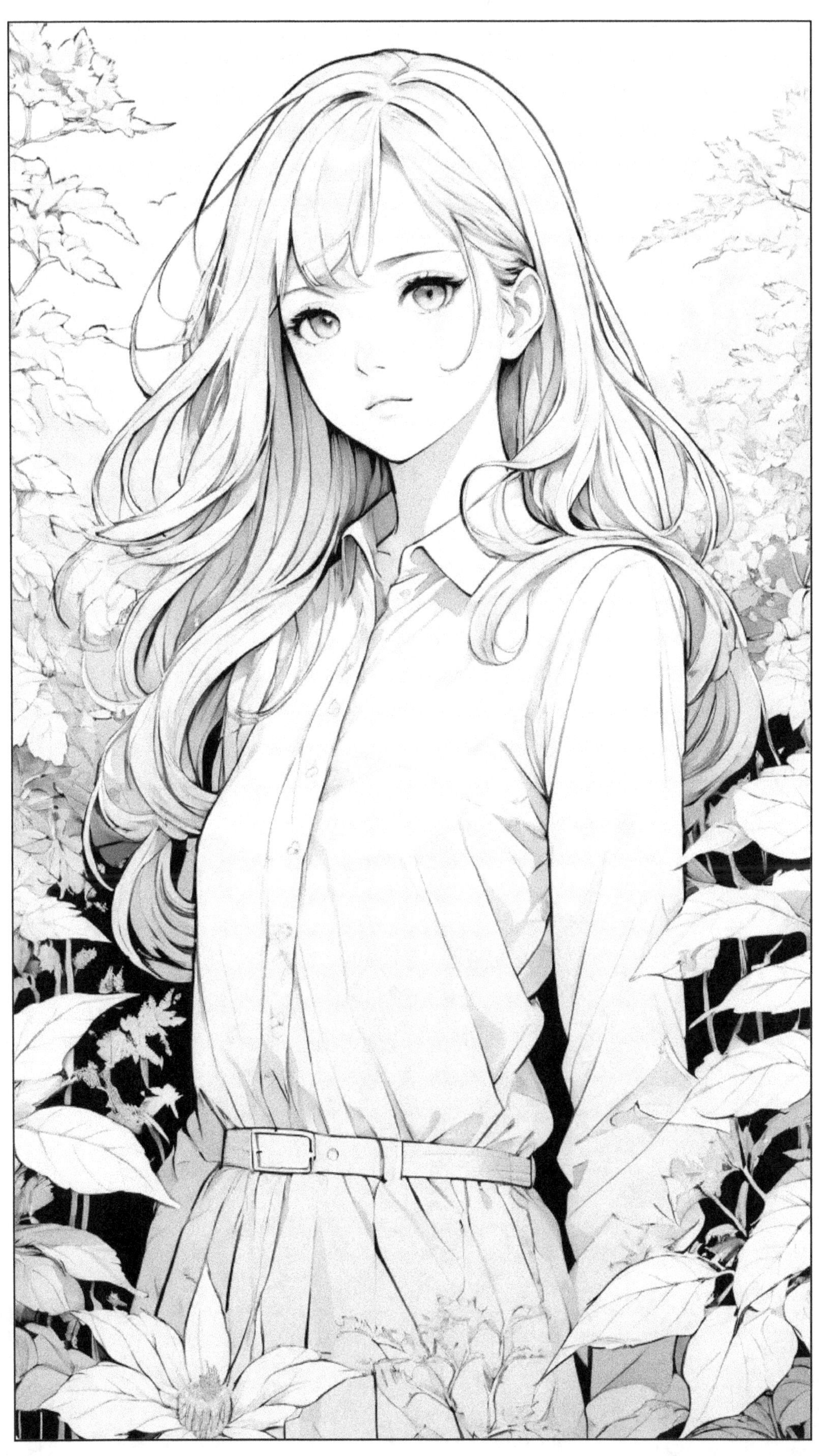

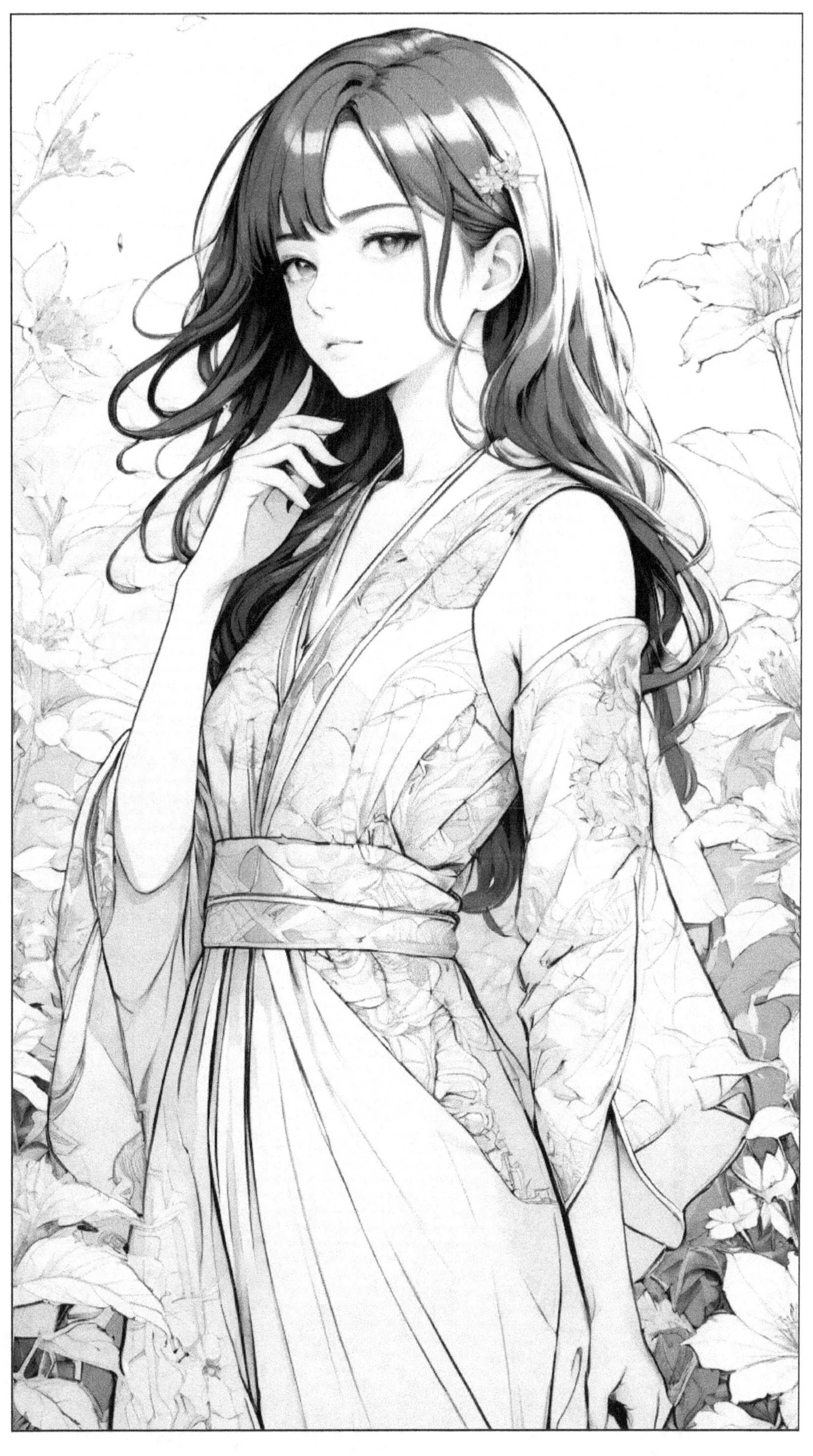

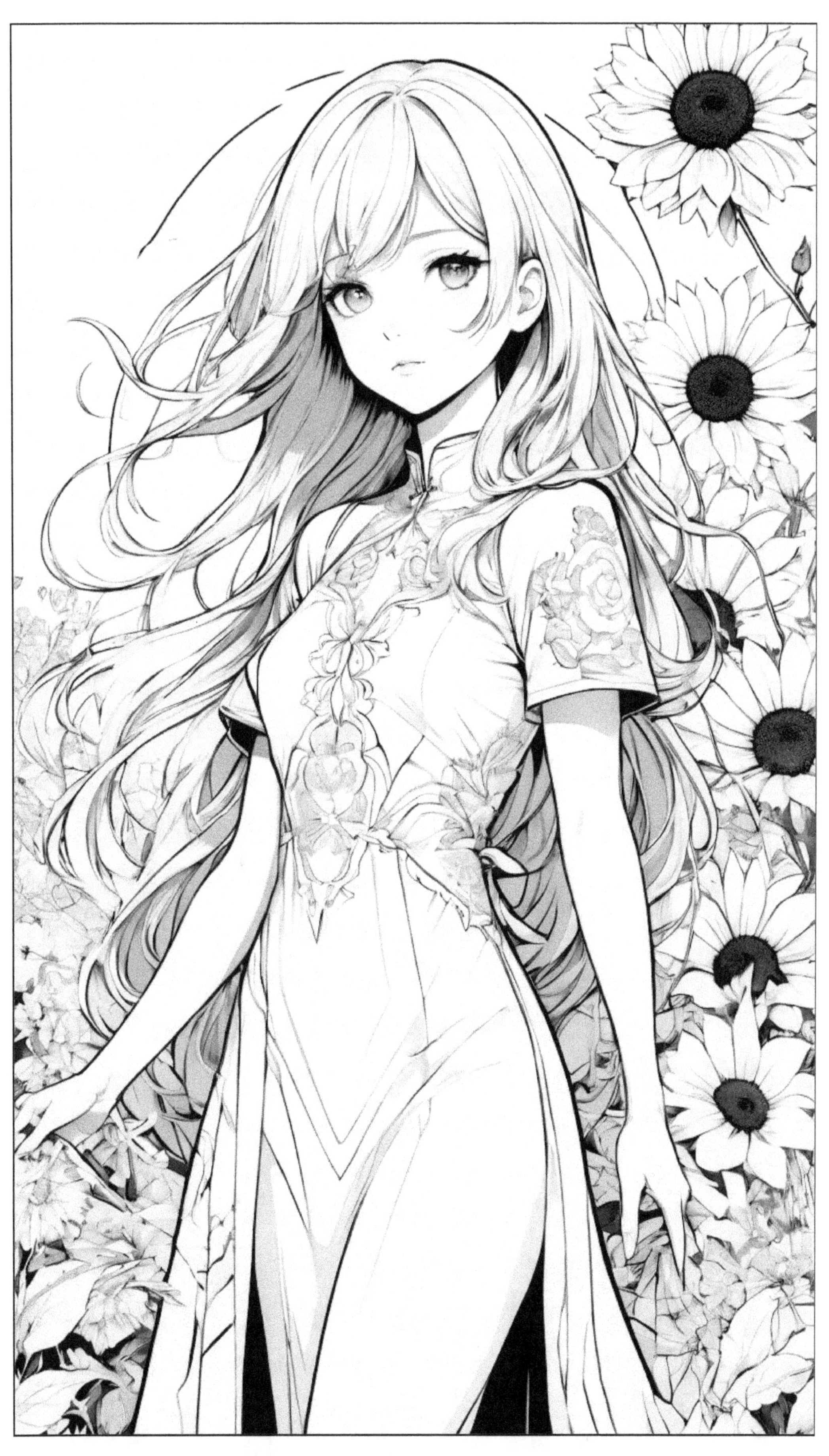

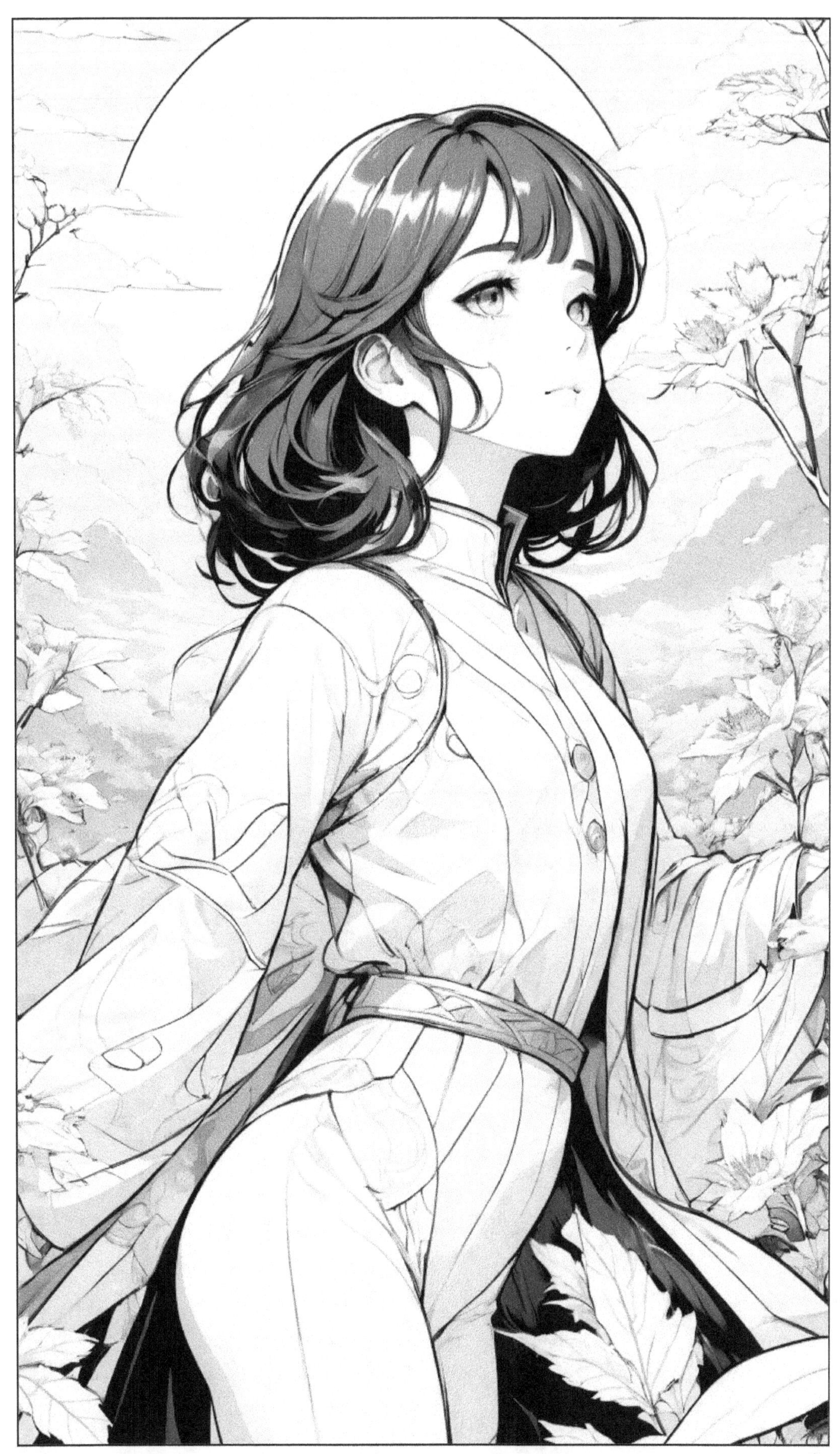

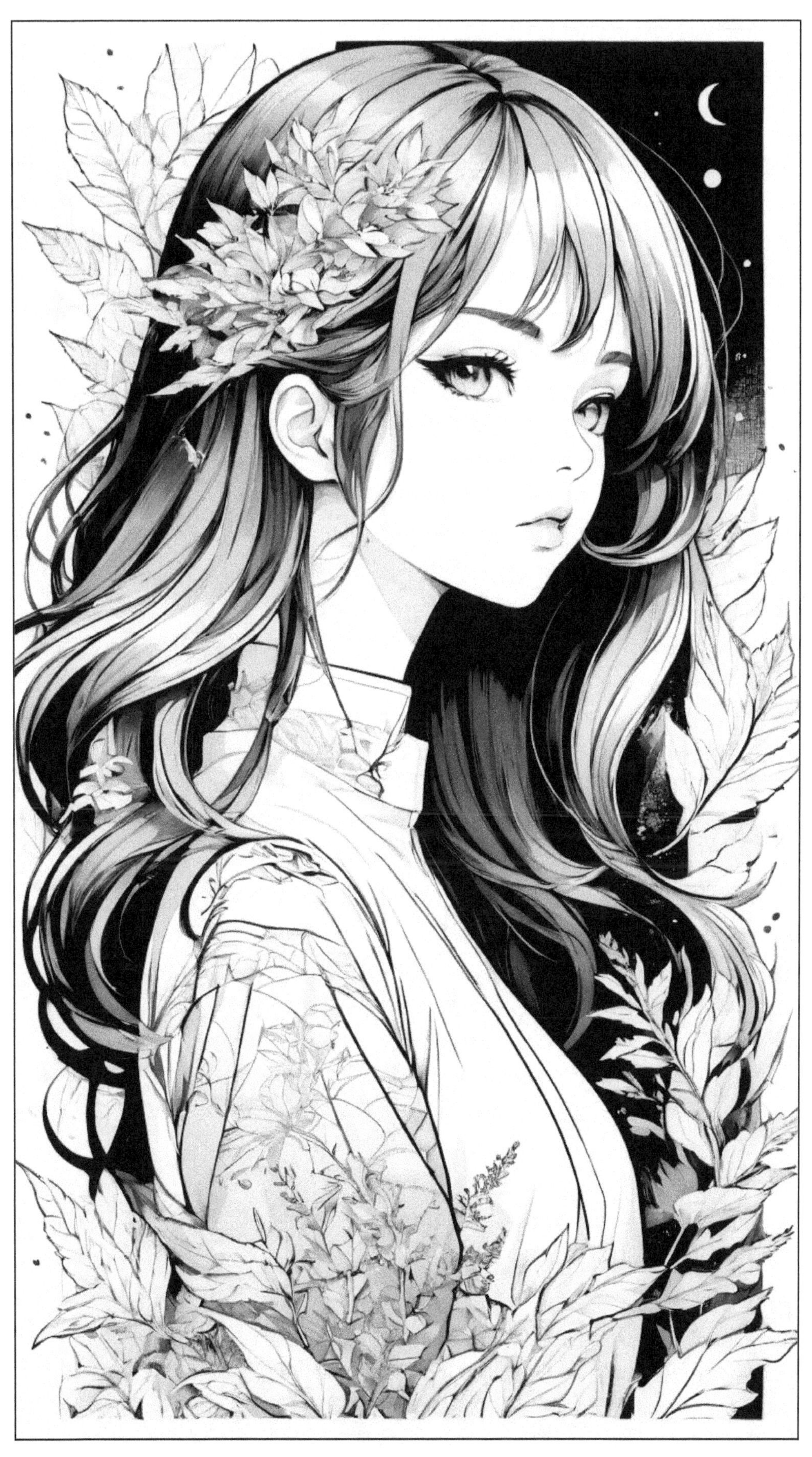

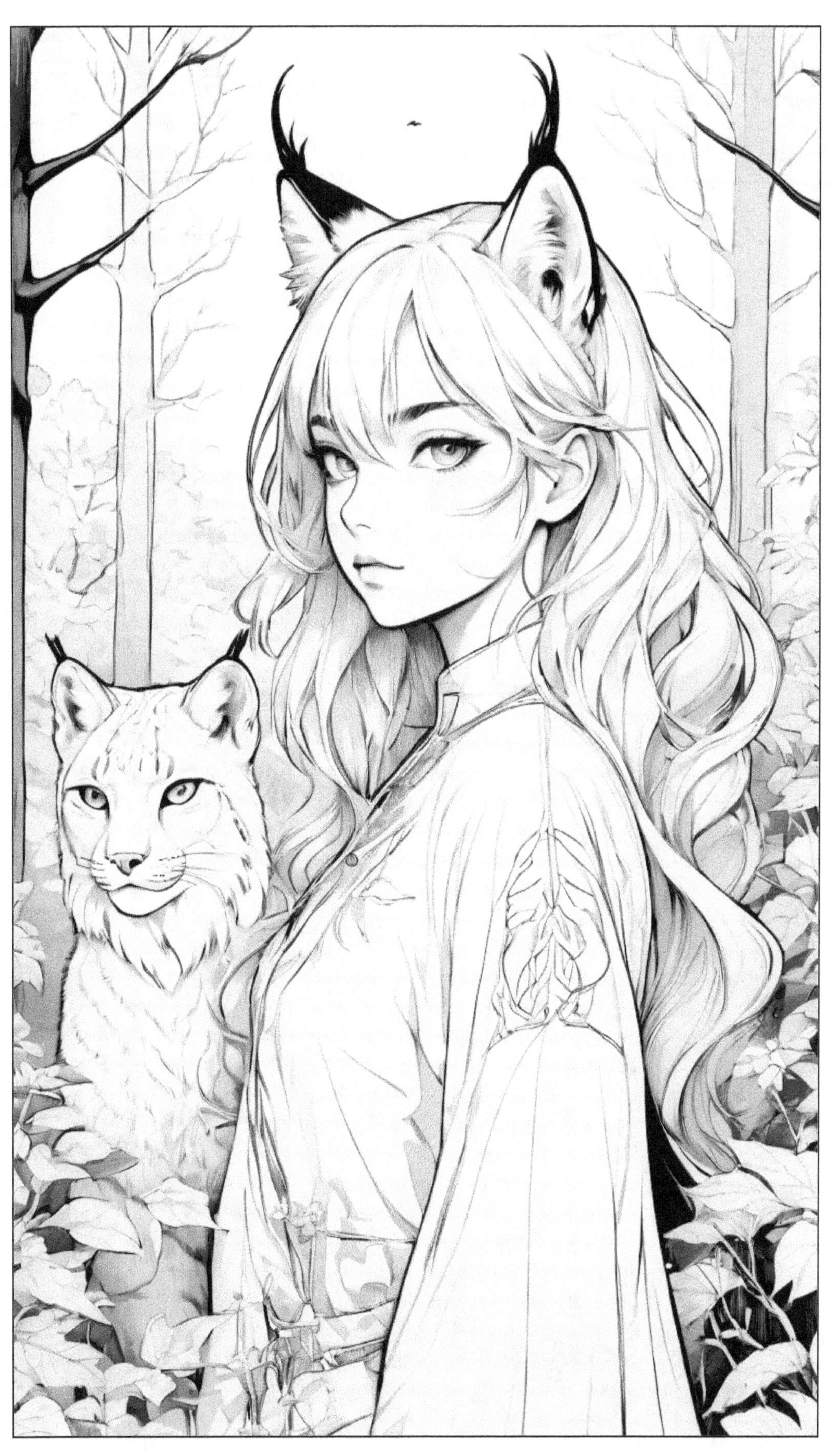

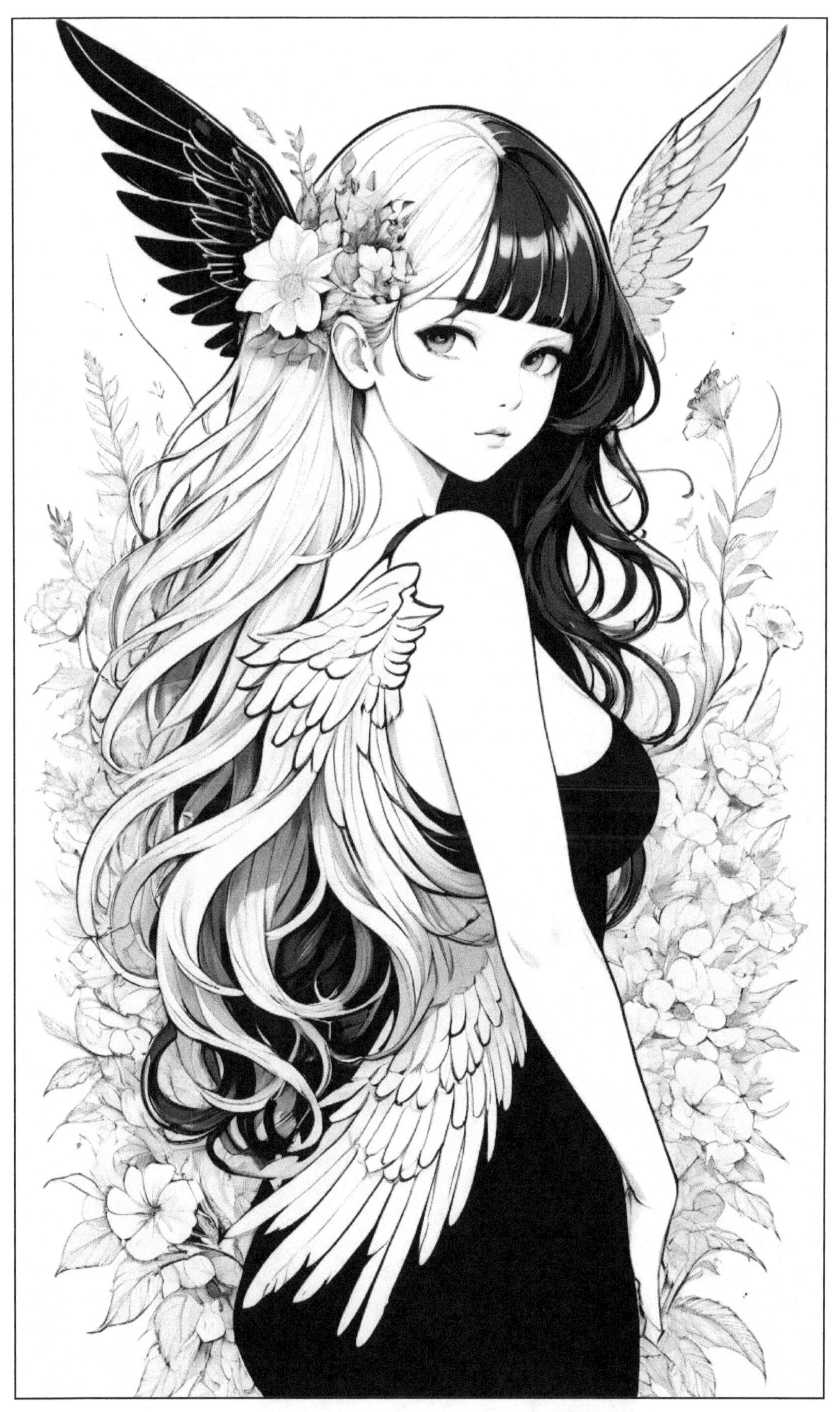

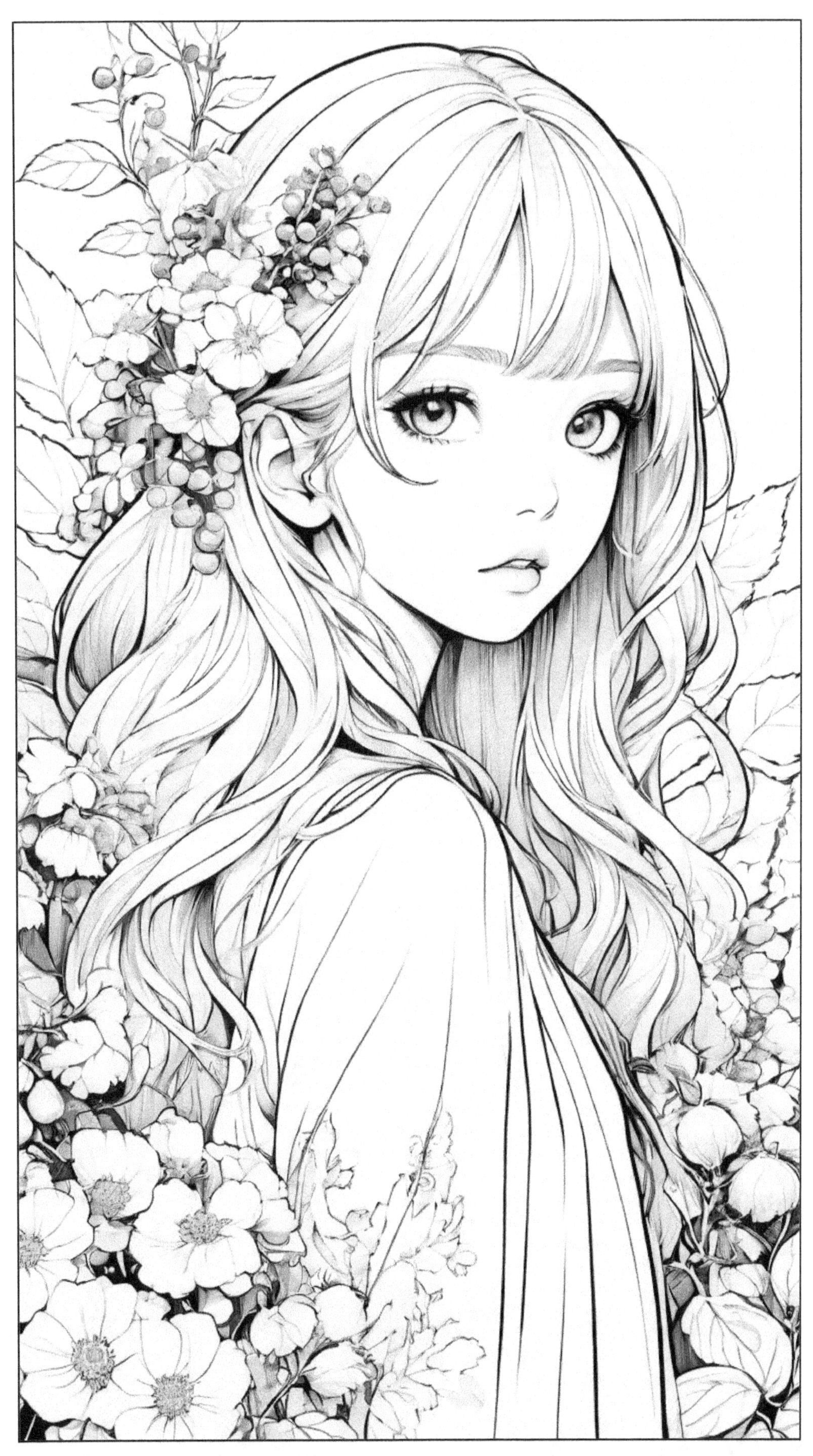

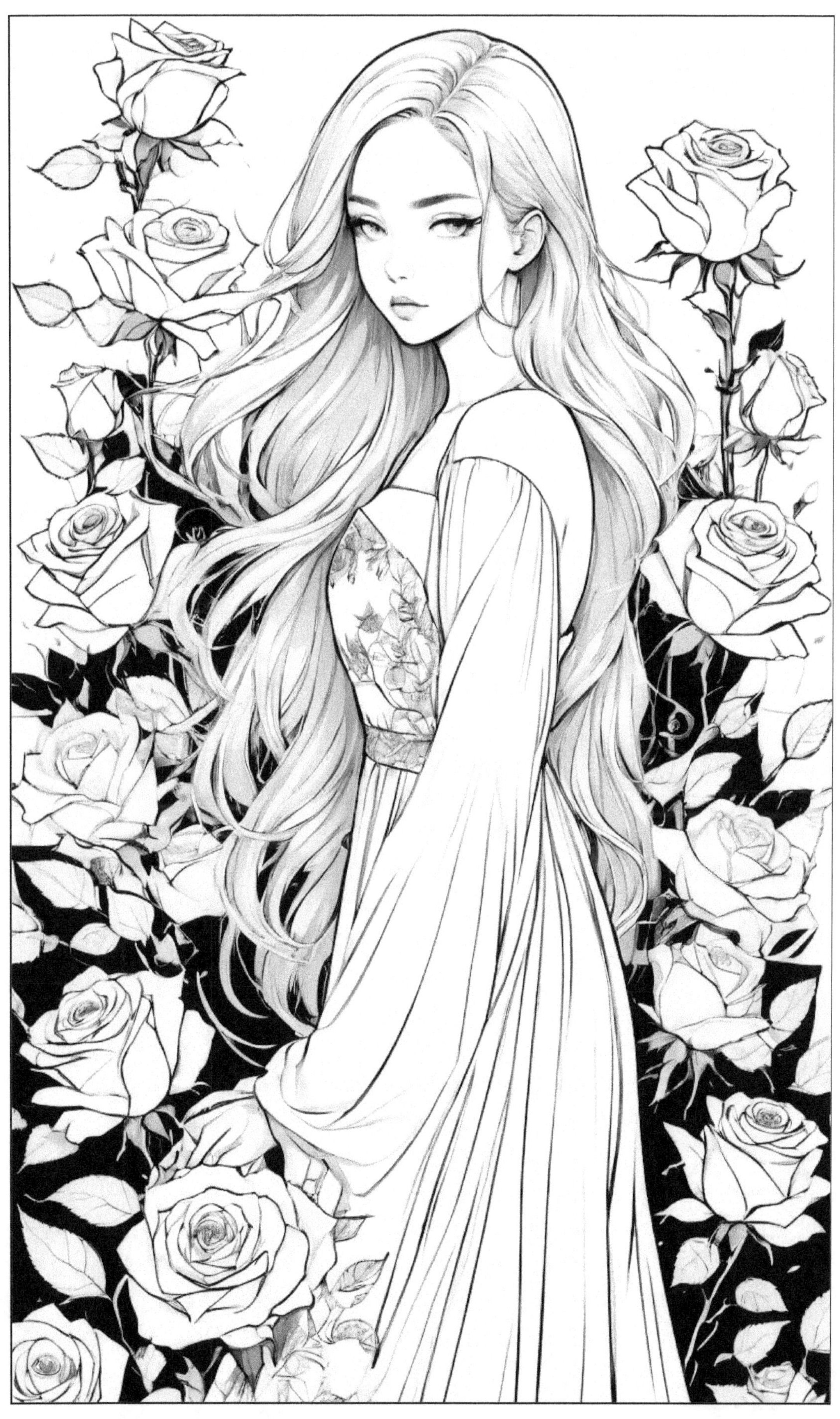

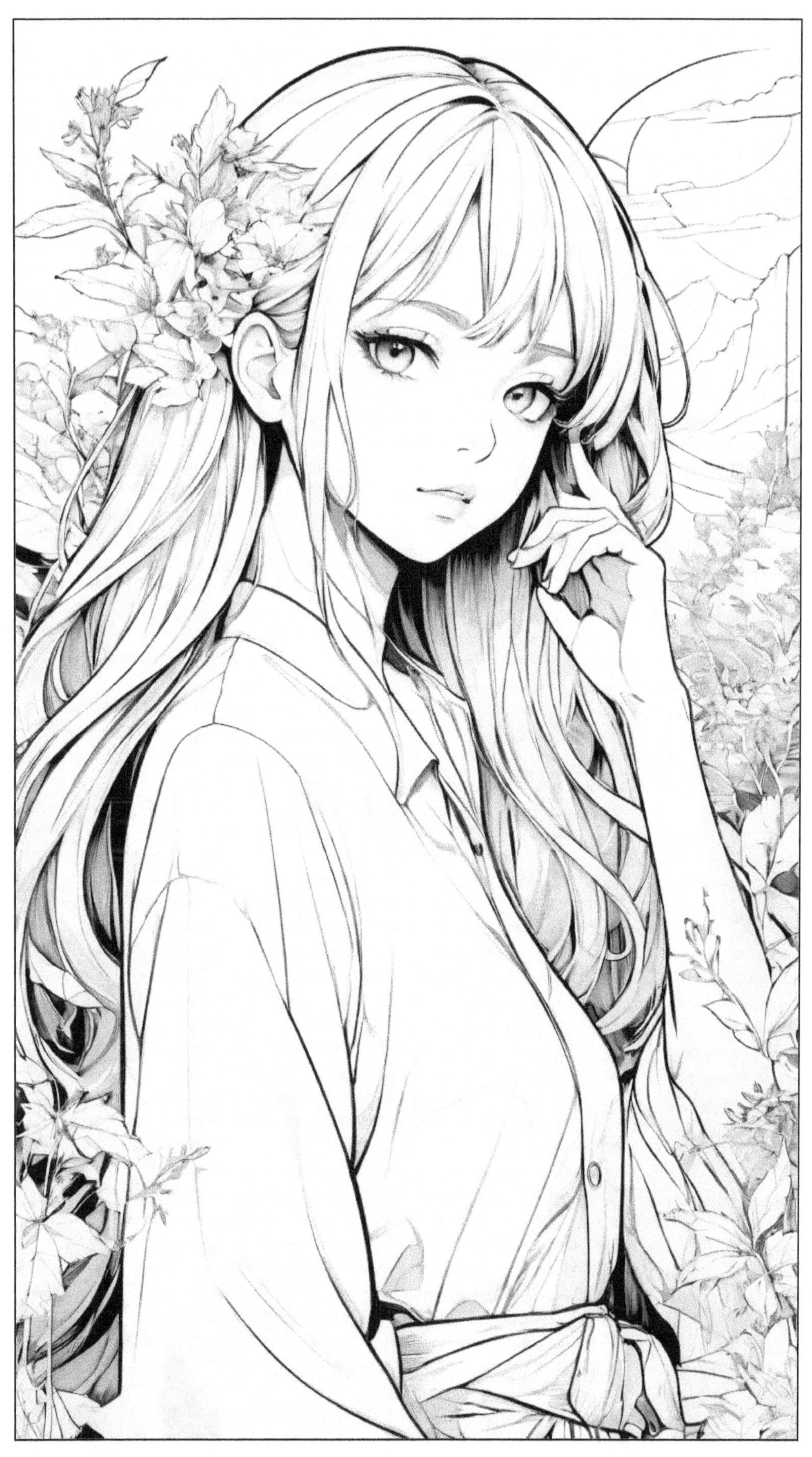

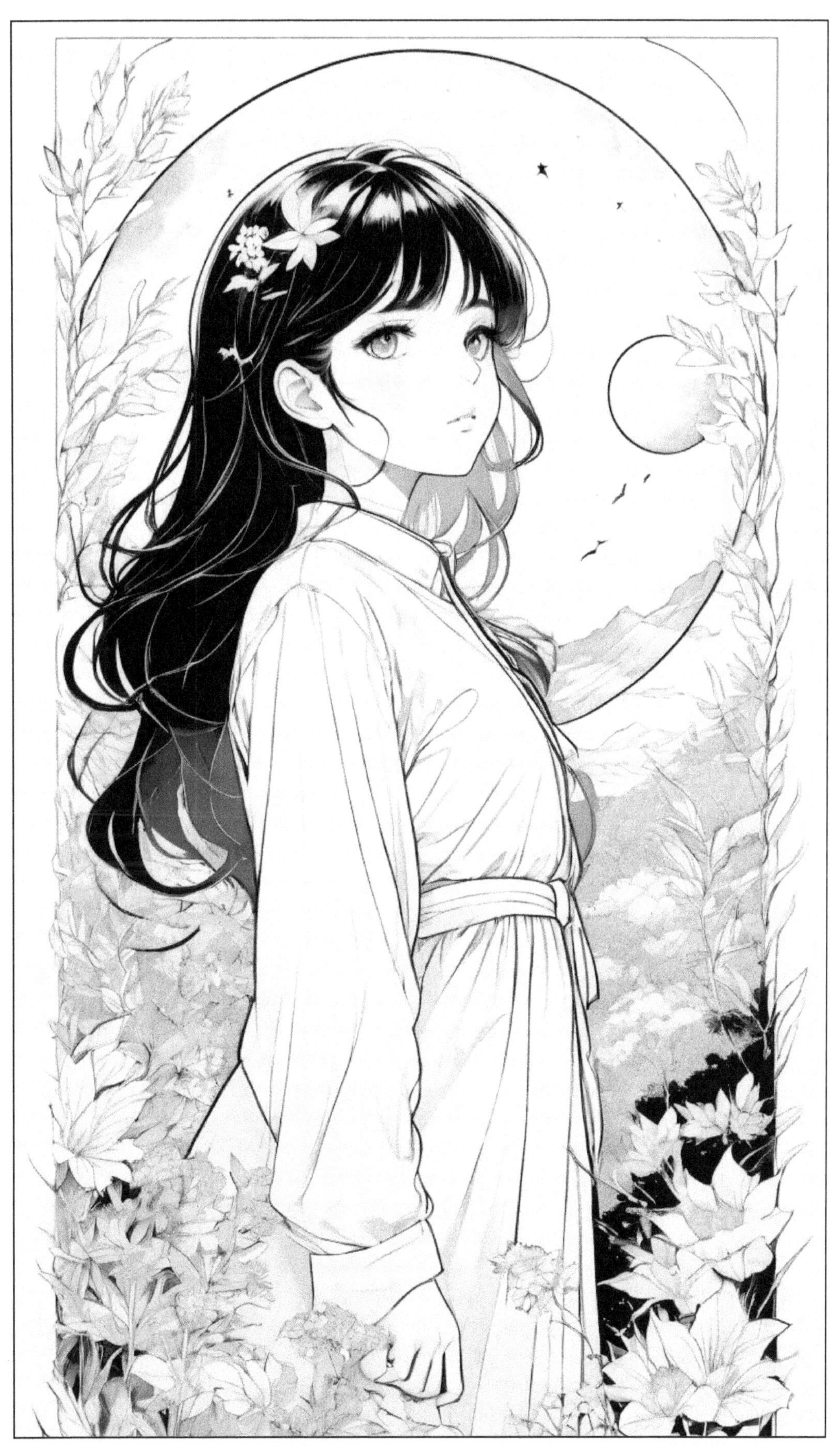

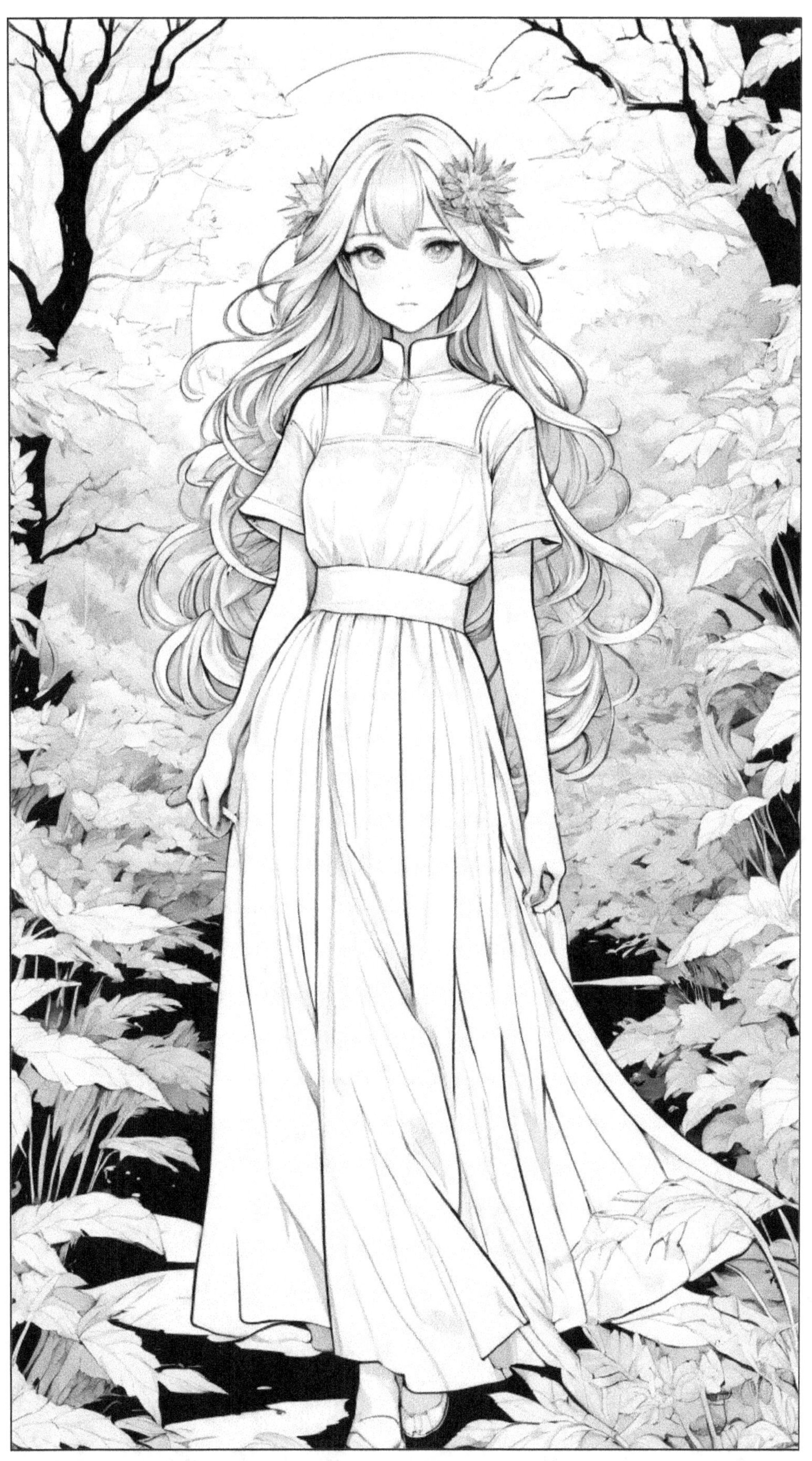

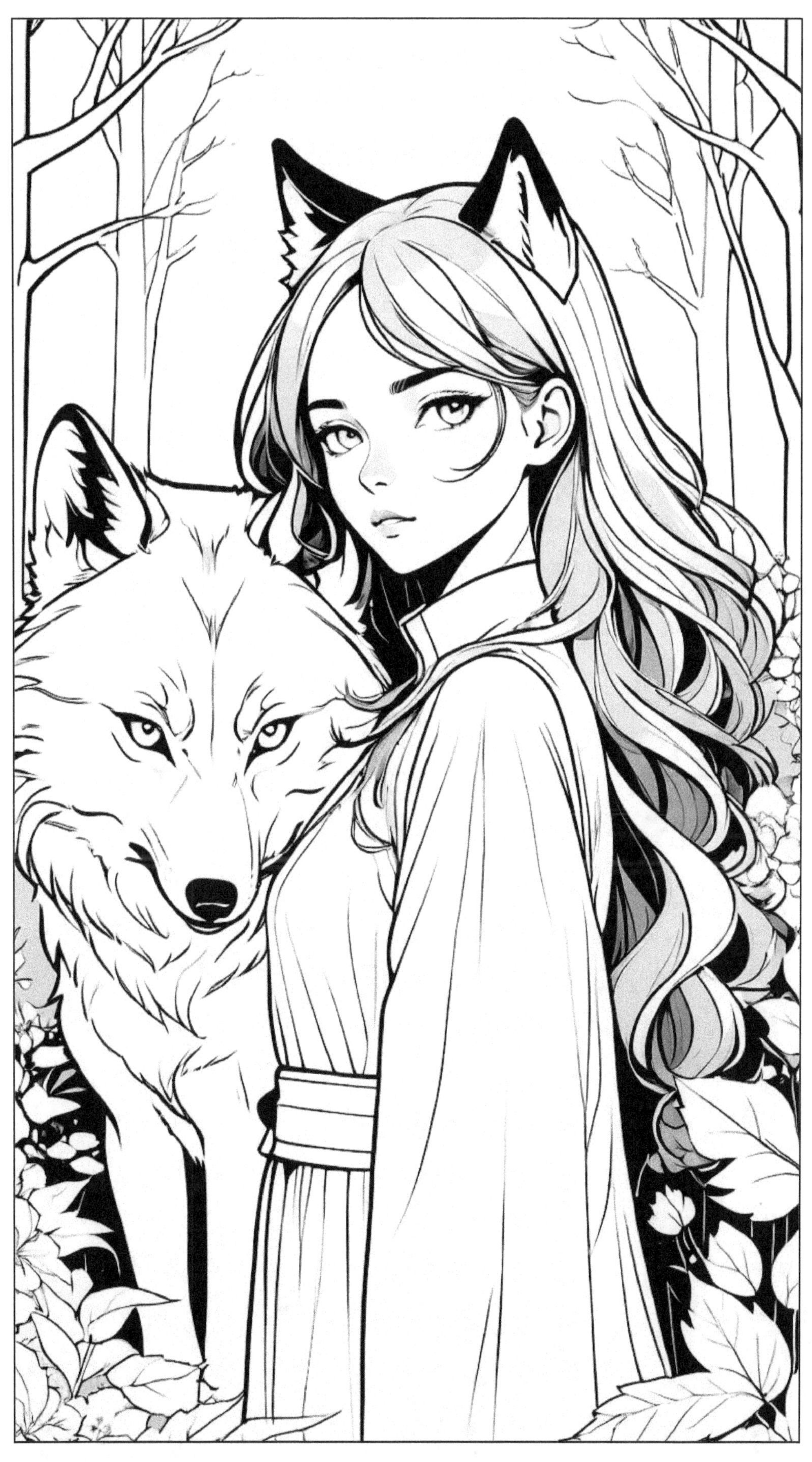

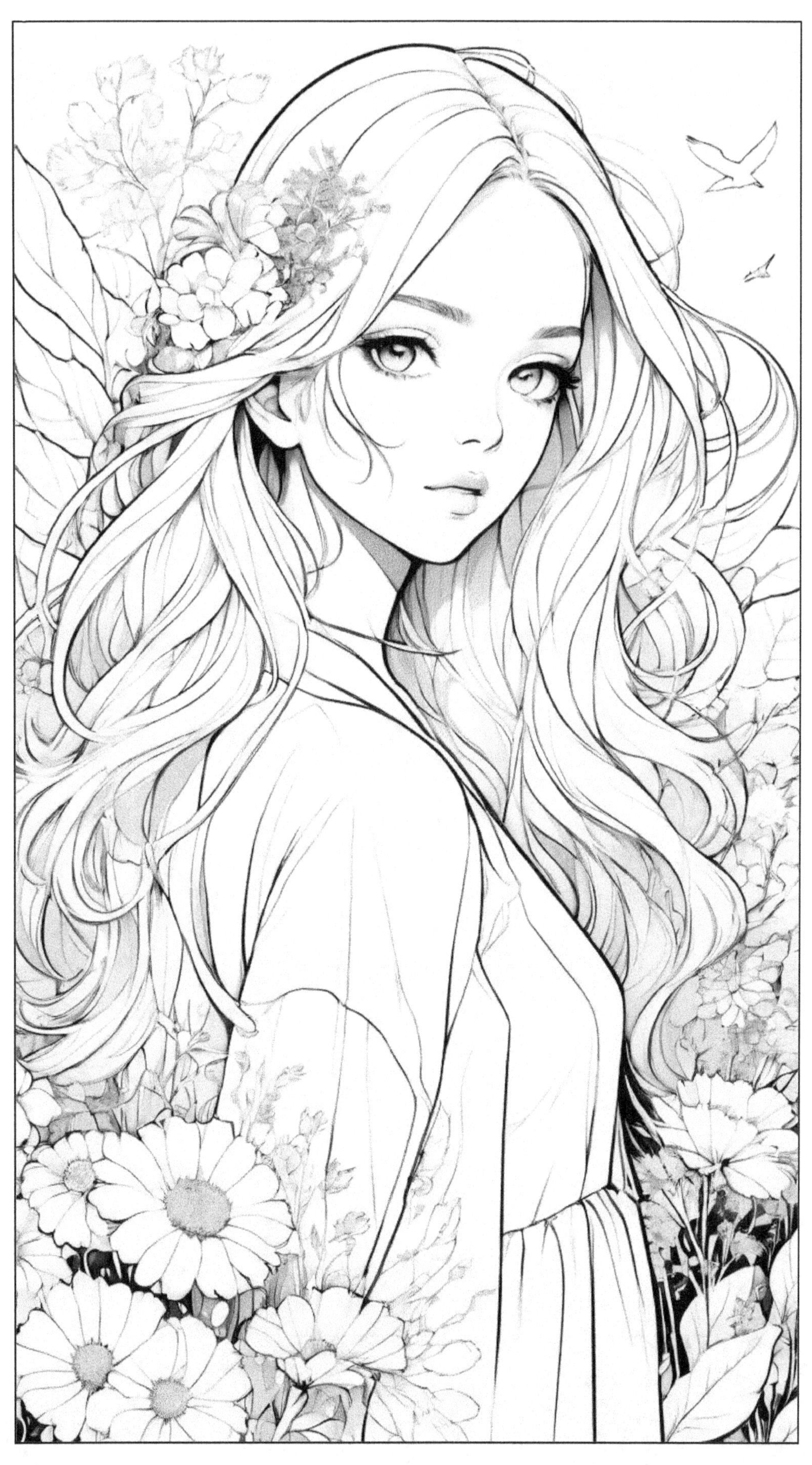

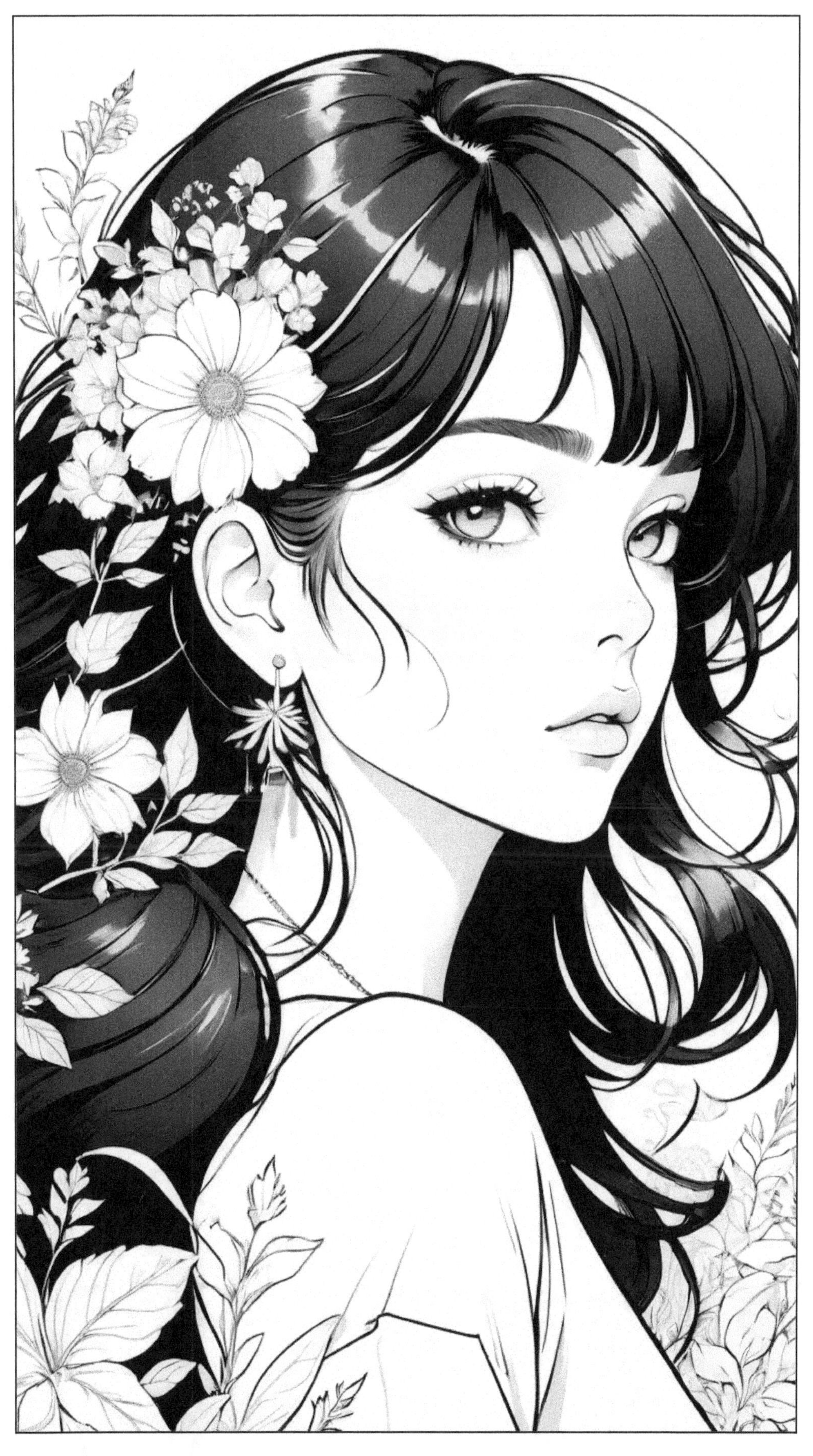

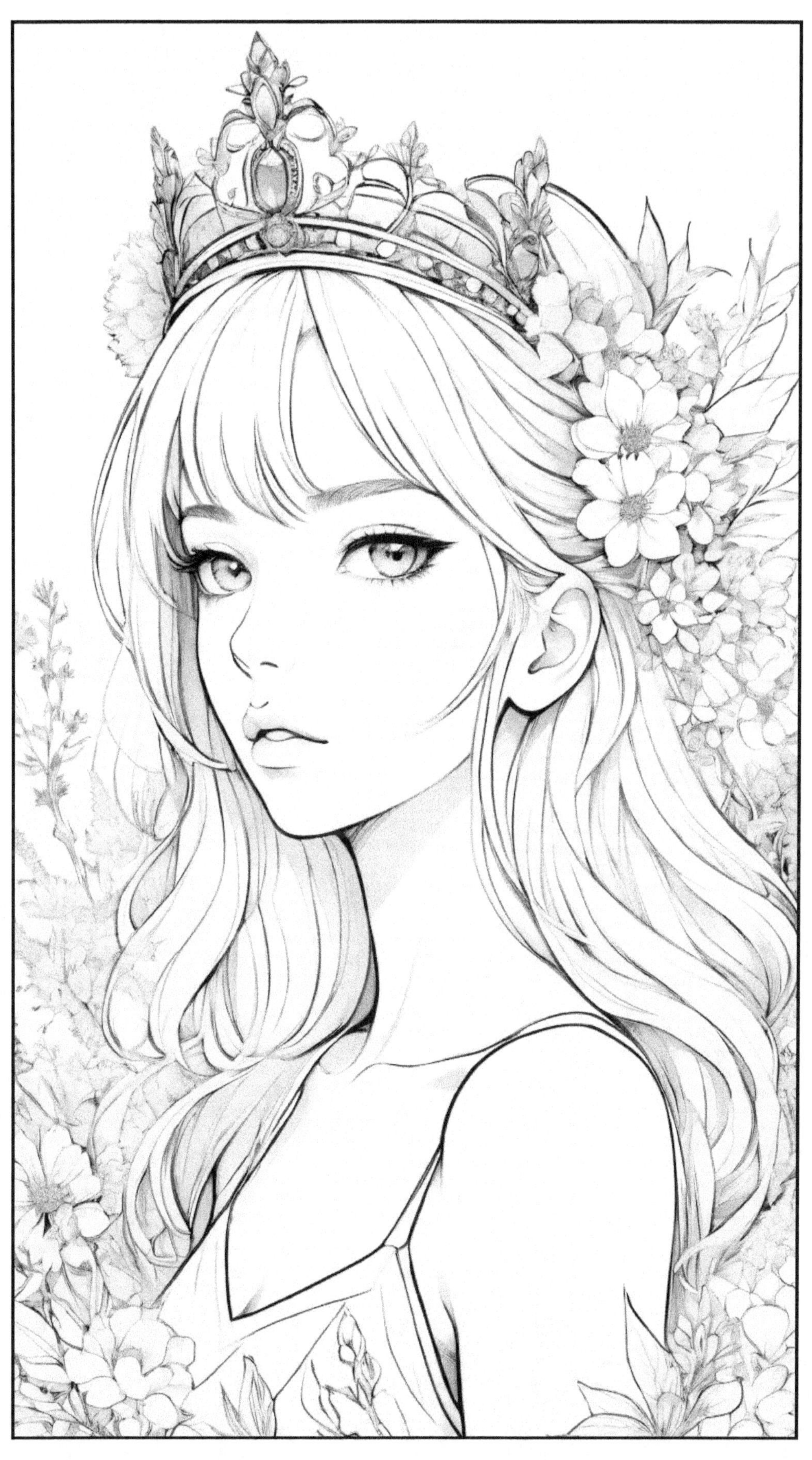

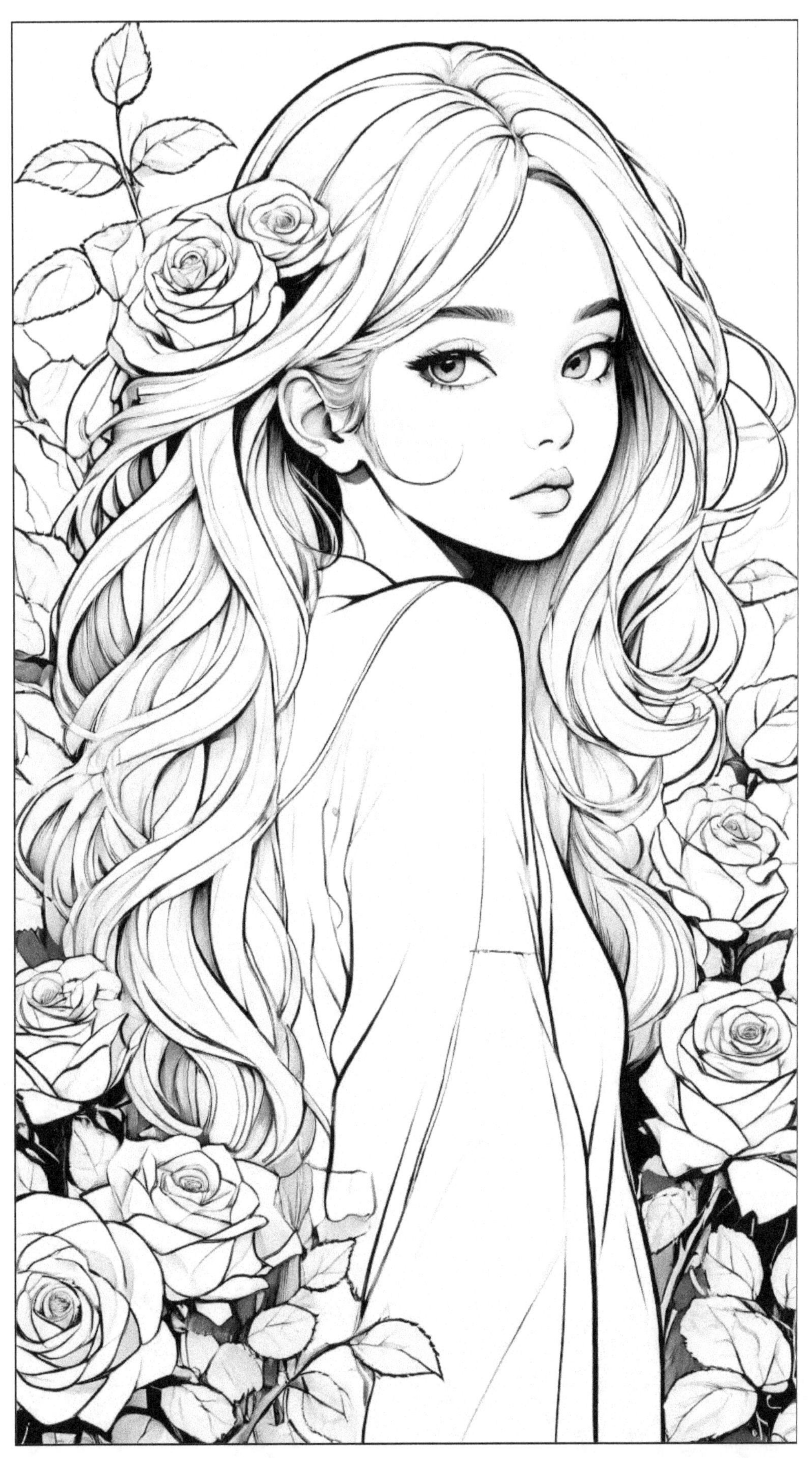

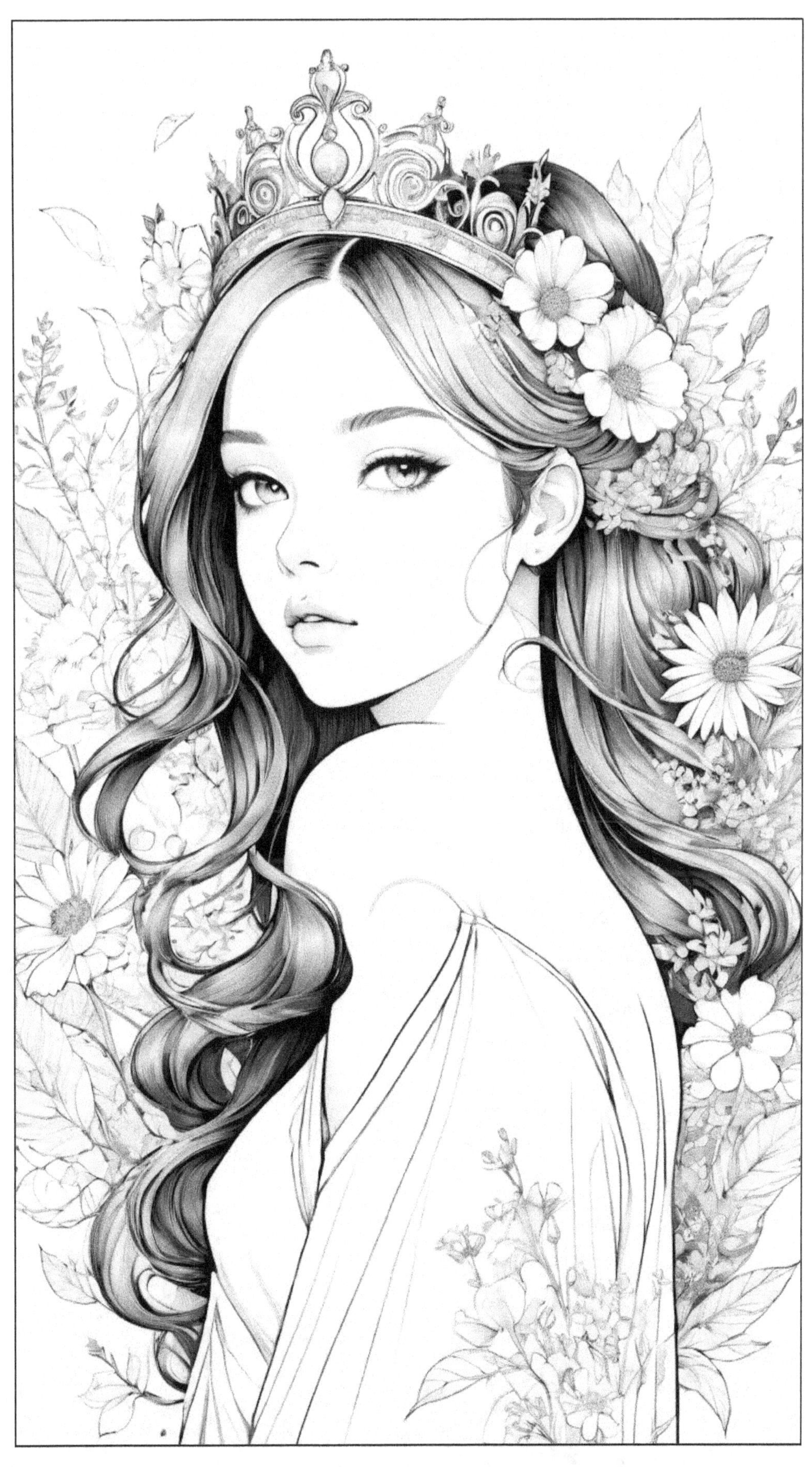

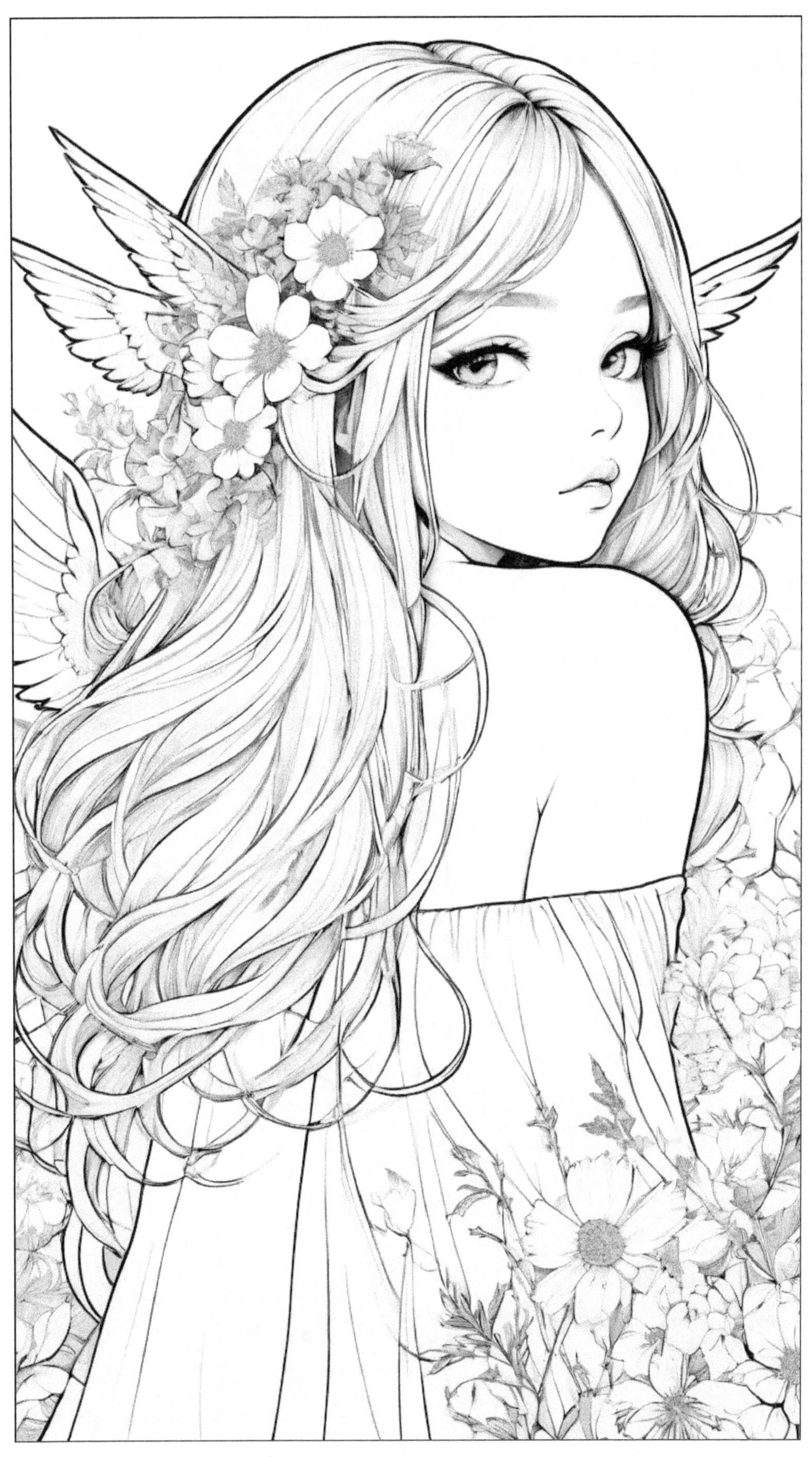

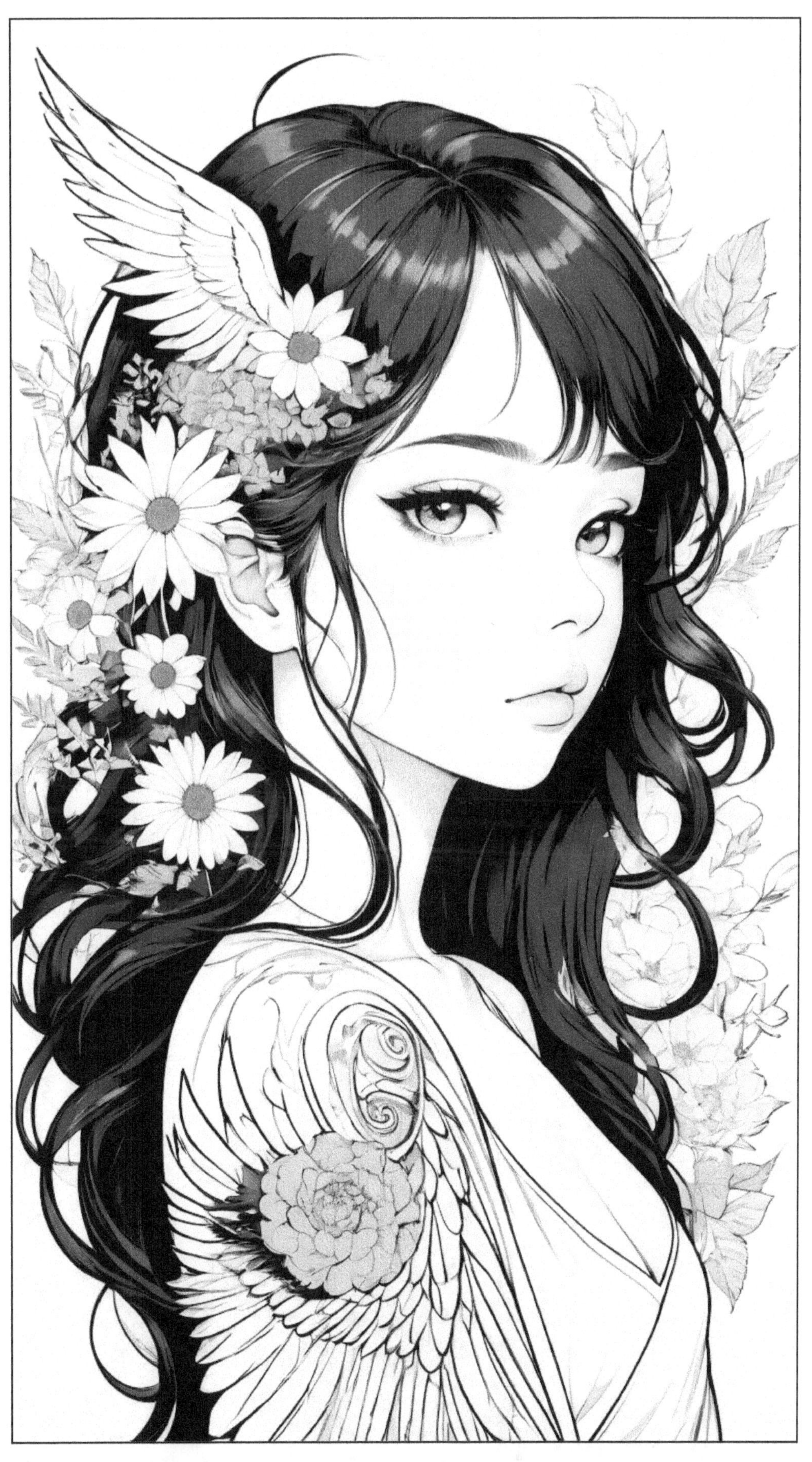

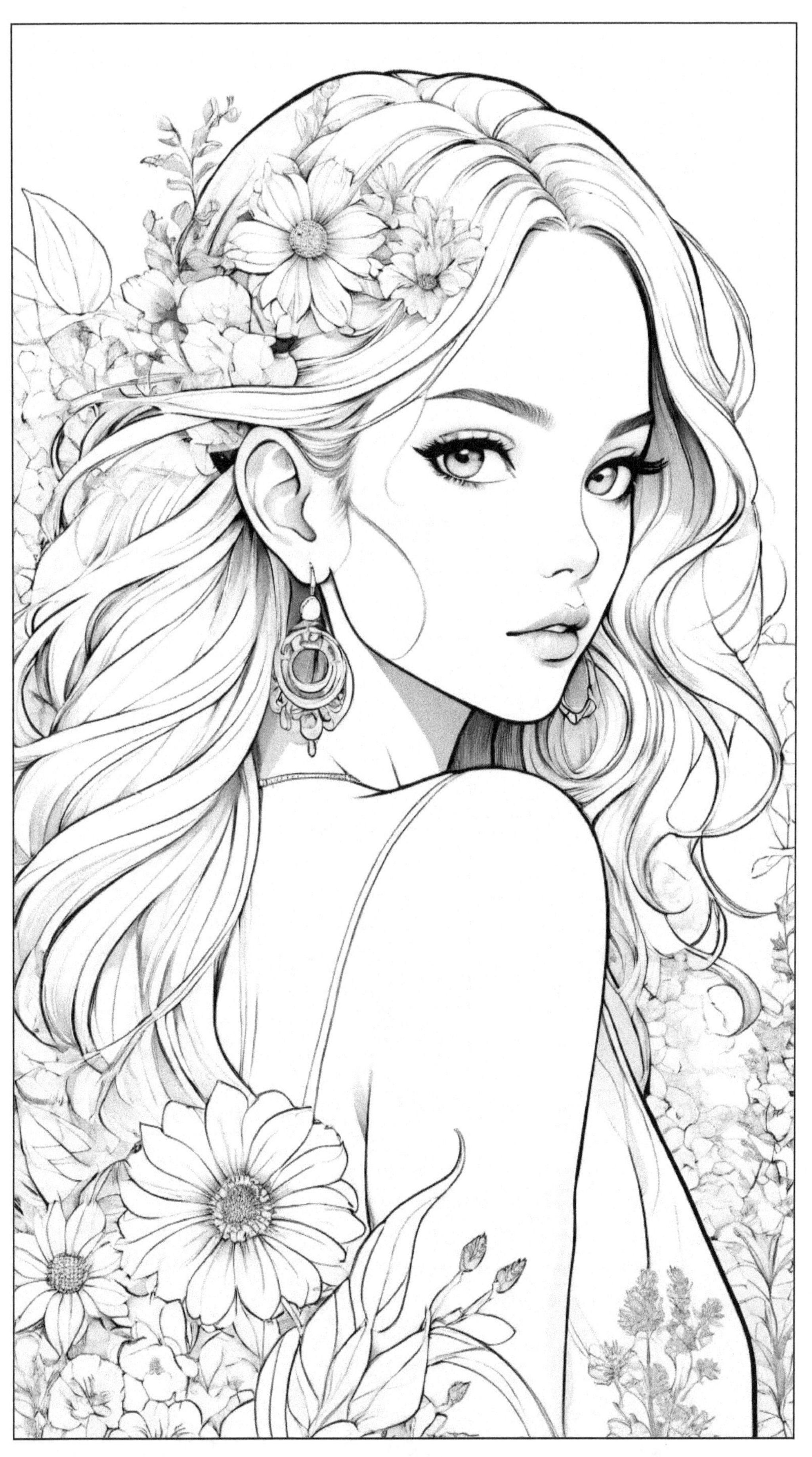